# Horizon Fev
## A E Filby

**Explorer A E Filby's own account of his extraordinary expedition through Africa, 1931 - 1935**

Collated and edited by
Victoria & Joe Twead

Photographs by A E Filby

Paperback Published in 2012 by Feedaread
Ebook Published by AntPress.org

First Edition

A CIP catalogue record for this title is available from the British Library.

**Books by Victoria Twead**
Chickens, Mules and Two Old Fools
Two Old Fools - Olé!
Two Old Fools on a Camel
Mouth-Watering Spanish Recipes
Morgan and the Martians (playscript)
Horizon Fever

# Acknowledgements

My heartfelt thanks must go to the following people:

My grandfather, **Edmund 'Solly' Filby,** whom I never met, for lovingly completing and safe-guarding Archie's scrapbooks following his son's early death. What terrible pain he must have felt as he pasted photographs and typed captions. Without these volumes, I would never have known the background to *Horizon Fever*, or seen actual photographs of the events described. Without Solly, I wouldn't have been able to share Archie's extraordinary adventures with the world.

**Phil Filby** and his sons, **Matthew, Alexander and Sebastian** for painstakingly photographing every page of Uncle Archie's 14 scrapbooks.

My brilliant son, **Shealan,** for the fabulous cover he designed. Yes, this book really is a family affair...

And, of course, **Joe,** who typed the whole manuscript and catalogued every photograph.

# Table of Contents

# Uncle Archie and his Manuscript

Archibald Edmund Filby, proclaimed "the World's most travelled motorist", was my uncle. He died before I was born and my father, naturally taciturn, rarely discussed his older brother.

My parents died in 1993, and I inherited a strange-looking and aged manuscript. Without looking inside, I filed it away for future consideration. I had, after all, my own young family to raise and it would be another 20 years (80 since the expedition) before the manuscript would again see the light of day.

"Look what I found!" I said excitedly to Joe, brandishing the manuscript. We'd already collaborated in other books I'd written; *Chickens, Mules and Two Old Fools* and its sequels.

"I guess I'd better start typing," muttered Joe.

Three months later, he had transcribed the four hundred-page document.

The result is a book that reveals a bygone age. The British Empire was in decline but remnants remained. The 'All-Red' route, to which Archie frequently refers, indicates the red colour cartographers used to denote British-controlled countries on maps.

Attitudes in those days were very different and often shocking. For instance, big game hunting was popular. Archie refers to adult Africans as 'boys' or 'natives'. On one occasion an Egyptian guard is treated with unconscionable thoughtlessness, which would horrify us today. Despite this, Archie's affection and respect for the indigenous populace cannot be disputed. He is clearly fascinated by the languages, customs and cultures of the African tribes he encountered - from pygmies in the Congo to the Masai in Central Africa.

We changed nothing of the original manuscript. It is exactly as Archie typed it in 1938, undoubtedly at the behest of his newly-wedded wife, Miss Fay Taylor, also a writer, whom he met following a radio broadcast he made from London. Sadly, their marriage was to become a tragic love story, described in the last pages of this book.

I make no apologies for the quality of the photographs. Apart from a few, the photos are Archie's, taken more than 80 years ago. One can only imagine the difficulties he encountered in recording his travels using only primitive camera equipment. Most of the captions beneath the pictures are Archie's own.

I began by saying I never knew my Uncle Archie. Now I feel I do. I regret not having met him in life, but his spirit lives on. Archie comes across as a courageous, feisty, quick-tempered, bossy little man, but full of fun, generous and never one to bear a grudge. I imagine his companions found him difficult to travel with, but he made friends easily and was much in demand by the Press and for radio and early television broadcasts.

One final thought... Archie had little money. The trip to Cape Town, in 1931, began in an ancient, sawn-in-half Rolls Royce, and was completed four years later in a 1922 Austin 20, the most modern of the four cars employed for the trip. The four thousand miles from Kenya to South Africa, undertaken in a Model T Ford considered vintage even in 1931, is a testament to the car manufacturer, especially when one considers the appalling condition of the roads in Africa at that time.

And so, without further ado, I hand over the story-telling to Uncle Archie.

**Victoria Twead**
**July 2012**

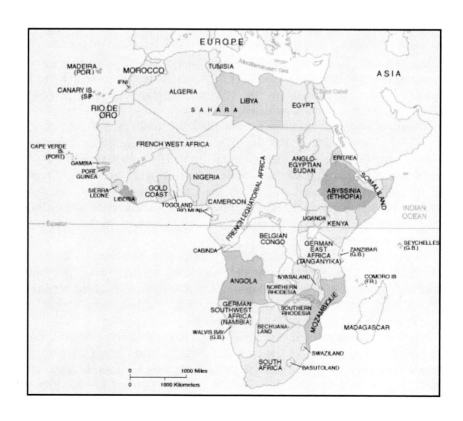

*Fay Filby*

**TO PETER FAYE**
**without whom this would never have been written**
[This dedication is to Archie's bride, Fay, who wrote under
the pen name of Peter Fayne]

**To save criticism from those who know, I should explain that
place-names, etc., were given to me by you who live there or
your predecessors.**

Archibald Edmund Filby
London, January 1938

# Chapter 1 ~ England, February 1931

"Adventure comes to the adventurous" is probably a true saying, but you cannot be an explorer until you have explored. I wanted to be an explorer. I'm sure that thought has been behind my mad rushing about, though up to now my best effort has been to be called "Explorado" on my papers in Angola. My latest passport announces that I am a journalist. Noncommittal, but on the right lines, I think.

It has, however, taken twenty years to get so far, if I don't count four years of war service, mostly done when I was well under the right age, during which I was always thrown out of the front line and told to report back at some base I could never find.

*[Archie lied about his age and enlisted in 1914, at 14½ years old]*

Then there were my adventures in Australia, where I rode in a buckjumping show, became entertainment manager for a leading hotel, ran a successful theatre, became a racing driver, and eventually went pearling in the Torres Straits and Coral Sea.

This was adventure, but not exploring, so I fitted out an expedition and tried to follow Leichardt's tracks into the back blocks of Australia known as the Never-Never, the net result being that I killed some good horses and brought my partner back tied up; a raving lunatic.

A pioneer run up Cape York to Thursday Island, better known as "T. I.", proved to me that I had much more possibility of success operating on my own. In spite of this I again teamed up this time for a voyage up the Fly River and a trip into the interior of New Guinea, only to bring my partner back wounded by a poisoned arrow and later to fight a duel over it with a naval officer on the shores of T. I.

Afterwards came a trip on a junk through the Arafura, Banda and Flores seas, and so eventually to Singapore; then in succession came India, Ceylon, China, Japan, the Dutch East Indies, and on and on, but always someone had been there first - in fact many people had been there. But darkest Africa was calling - avidly I read up books that stressed the Ju-Ju playing the tom-tom or the Tom-Tom playing the Ju-Ju, I wasn't sure which was which, but it was obviously the place to go exploring and thus an African safari was born.

Now, it's not much good being an explorer if nobody knows you are one, and therefore a good Press is necessary. I had several friends in Fleet Street, and I tried it out on them, casually - "You know I'm off to Africa, exploring." No-one seemed interested, but a few people offered the idea that I might fly to Capetown in record time, say three or four days - oh, there was a story. But, hang it all, you can't explore the Dark Continent in four days, so I decided on a car.

In one respect I was on a par with those who had set out on the rocky path of exploration and had eventually become famous - lack of finance - and it was obvious that I couldn't do anything really worth while on my capital of five pounds; but I told myself it was only necessary to find a backer and the shekels would roll in. The trouble was, though, to meet one. Letters were useless; I'd always been a good talker and I wanted to get hold of my man and work up his enthusiasm. I knew some members of my club were big game hunters, and had the finance to back an adventure if they wished, and I decided to try it on one of them.

I was lucky enough to find the very man I wanted, and having walked up and down the lounge muttering darkly to myself and rehearsing my opening gambit, I marched into the bar and sat on a high stool waiting for my prey to come. Sure enough, in he came. I suggested a noggin, which he accepted, and I was off.

A casual opening, as befitted an old hand, would be best, I thought, so having fulfilled the rites of raising the glass and saying "Bung", I started.

"Going to the Dark Continent soon, you know."

"Where?"

"You know - Africa."

"Oh! By Jove, you will enjoy it! I know it pretty well. I must give you a chit to an old pal of mine in Jo'burg, keeps the most astounding private bar you ever saw - Vodka, Van der Hum, that Danish drink with bits of gold leaf floating about in it, and even audit ale. I bet you can't name a drink he hasn't got."

"But I'm not going to civilised parts. I'm off to the little-known interior - Ituri Forest, pygmies, and all that."

"Pity, you should have met this bloke. Solomon, I think that's his name; everyone knows him as Uncle. Knows all the show girls, too. Have a spot?"

"Thanks. No, I intend to do a spot of exploring, go in by way of Lobite and work through the Ituri - you know, the Ituri Forest - biggest in the world - and make for Stanleyville."

"Stanleyville? That's not a bad spot. I went on a pub crawl there. 'Member getting some rather decent Portuguese wine which we had with a bath-load of mussels sent up from the coast - you should try 'em when you get there. Well, I'm off - just packing up and going to do some shooting in South America. Taking a chap with wads of cash, so should have some fun."

Next day I visited the Headquarters of the Overseas League, where I met John Parker, a six-footer with that indefinable colonial stamp, who had, so he told me, spent some years in South Africa and Northern Rhodesia. During the course of a few drinks, the idea of the British Trade Development Expedition was born, the scheme being to gather together a number of firms and act as representatives for them. Samples would be carried and agents appointed, the route being from Cairo to Capetown, and the method of transport a car.

This, of course, was not exactly what I had in mind, but it seemed to offer a possibility of getting some finance together, and of landing me in the Dark Continent.

During the morning I was introduced to Mr. Eric Rice, one of the Travelling Secretaries of the Overseas League, and he made the suggestion that we should represent the League on a run from Vernon House, London to Rhodes House, Capetown, to celebrate the League's twenty-first birthday, also to enrol members en route. He also suggested that as there were many advertisers in the League Magazine, "Overseas", who might be represented, we should use the editorial office and work from there.

This was "off" with a vengeance. I was introduced to Sir Evelyn Wrench, the founder of the League, who gave the scheme his blessing and made some more useful suggestions.

With practically no capital, it meant a terrific amount of work, but we had the office, borrowed a typewriter, and got down to it. John Parker luckily was a good typist, and I soon had him hard at it, while I interviewed firm after firm with a fair number of successes.

In the morning I would draft out a number of letters calculated to make manufacturers rush at us with fat cheques, and John would shape these to fit any enquiry, while I went out to interview those who were nibbling.

At midday we would repair to the Overseas Club bar, where we received advice from everyone who had ever left the shores of England. Little of it proved of much value to us, but there must have been a steady rise in the bar receipts.

One day Rice produced the third member of our party, who turned out to be half French and half Australian, beautifully dressed, with the correct bowler and the permanently rolled umbrella, all set off with by a fine Guardsman's moustache. Adding to the effect was the most curious collar I had ever seen, with points stuck straight out from his neck, which to my eye spoilt the general ensemble. It was not until we were well down in the desert that I learnt he was wearing duelling shirts, the only ones he had.

Not knowing this at the time, I wasn't very favourably impressed, but when we heard he was in receipt of a permanent income, besides being put forward by our main sponsors, the League, he was pressed into service. Useful with a typewriter, and possessing the charm of his French heritage and the directness of his Australian, his excellent line of sales talk proved a valuable asset in persuading reluctant firms.

*Me, John and Teddy*

We still hadn't got a car, but funds were beginning to come in, and one day, in our source of inspiration, the bar, we found someone who had a 40/50 Rolls for sale at a figure we could almost manage.

Some eleven years before, it must have lorded it round town with its huge coach body, then, getting more aged, it had been repainted and a larger radiator fitted, making it a most imposing equipage, but hardly the ideal for our safari. Yes, it had already got to "safari".

I set out to cultivate the owner with a view to getting the price down. Longer sessions at the bar were involved in this procedure, and led to a night when we ended up in the flat of an Indian princess, where I thoroughly disgraced myself by getting very tight and offering to bang together the heads of any or all of her feminine boyfriends. This put things back a little, but finally the deal went through and the car was ours.

I had my own ideas as to the kind of body I wanted, but the bar produced friends eager to introduce us to the leading body builders, who would assuredly cut their prices to nothing for us. So I went on a round of body builders. As soon as I mentioned Rolls and the trip they were off... "Yes of course, we know just what you want, Sir. We built a shooting brake for Lord X to use on his Scottish estate. Yes, here it is - £700. Of course we *could* cut that price for you, but if you want these other fixtures they would be extra, though we don't advise them. Lord X wrote to say how suitable his had been..."

Back to the bar for more inspiration, where I used up most of the club notepaper drawing up plans of the body I wanted and figuring costs, etc. Having got out the best design I could, the three of us went into conclave, and John said he knew someone in Kingston who he thought could do it. He came off the typewriter, took over our transport, and disappeared with it. His 'phone call during the day was not very encouraging, as he said he couldn't get the price down to anything like we wanted if we kept to my design of a cab in front and a sort of box body behind. So I gave instructions to get a crosscut saw and saw the blasted thing in half behind the driver's seat, leaving the cab, and to put a Cape cart effect on the back.

I never saw the body builder or knew his name, nor did I officiate at what must have been a sight to break the heart of a super coachbuilder, that is, the sawing in half of a Rolls Royce, but I take off my hat to John and his body builder, and the job cost exactly twenty-five pounds.

Things were moving smoothly, but we were nearly held up by the consequences of a farewell party given at what used to be the Belgravia Hotel. John, who had a very ancient Wolsely, ran us down from the club, and we were soon making merry. By the time midnight struck, the party dwindled, leaving John, myself and a retired South African judge, who was holding forth at great length on the beauties of South Africa, when suddenly I noticed that John had vanished.

I guessed that he had gone to the car, which we had left in the little street behind the hotel, and knowing how hard it was to start, and rather doubting his ability to drive after the party, I went round to bring him back. I found him swaying to and fro on the kerb, waving a half crown under an indignant policeman's nose and saying amiably, "Tha's a' ri', p'liceman, tha's a' ri'!"

With visions of us all being had up for bribery and corruption, I retrieved John and grabbed the half crown, and as we passed I put it into the policeman's pocket, not an easy job, as you will see if you look at a policeman's uniform.

As we returned to the hotel I was trying to work out whether I had laid myself open to a bribery charge, coming to the comforting conclusion that there was no law against putting half crowns in policemen's pockets.

Two more drinks and John was missing again. A reconnaissance proved that the car had also gone, so I made my way disconsolately back to the hotel once more.

The next I heard of him was a ring from Vine Street the next morning, and on arrival there, I got some details of what had happened. It seems that John had been trying to start up the car, but unfortunately he had been turning an imaginary handle and jiggling a non-existent throttle some ten yards in front of it, when he had been arrested, the charge being "drunk in charge of a car".

This was one of the first cases under a new law, and the A. A. had decided to make a test case of it, but to my mind went the wrong way about it in trying to prove that John was not drunk. His father, a Surgeon Rear Admiral and his uncle, a Harley Street specialist had, I found, visited him during the morning and said he was not drunk, but knowing John's powers of recovery, that didn't seem to disprove the theory of the police doctor that he was when he was brought in.

The case came up before Justice Mead, and I tried to convey that there was no harm in a man standing in a back street making handle-turning motions and saying "Brrrr!", but Justice Mead remarked that my evidence was so peculiar that it was better to omit it from the records.

So we lost the case and had to pay a large fine, while John could not drive for some months, in England at least.

*Der tag* was approaching fast, besides, not a lot, but enough, business was in, with plenty promised.

One day, Sir Evelyn Wrench sent for me and asked me to go to No. 10 Downing Street. This was fame indeed! I strutted into the famous portal and promptly got lost in the dingy corridor, from which I had to be rescued by a friendly charlady, who directed me to the august personage who wished to see me. [Ramsey MacDonald] Having answered a few questions regarding the safari, I was told to keep my eyes open and then was shown out again.

Two days to go, and Number Three, who suggested we should call him Teddy, but was more often called something far more virile, came to tell me that his remittance had not come and his landlady was threatening to get in touch with the League over two weeks' rent that was owing. I cleared that up on the understanding that we could draw on him at a later date if necessary.

Proudly John and I took the car round to be photographed outside the Vacuum Oil Company's premises in Tothill Street, as we were to use their products. We rather expected to draw an audience, but nobody seemed to realise we were the natural successors to the Merchant Adventurers. A few people eyed us curiously and eventually a most undiscerning policeman told us to move on.

I worked far into the night and had to go out to see one or two firms in the morning. On my return to the club I found a most satisfying crowd, also the movie people and about sixteen Press men with a battery of cameras. I rather suspect that the whisky samples we had on board and the open club bar were the main interest.

*Me, Teddy and John with the Rolls outside Vernon House*

Everyone drank everyone else's health, mostly in our samples, Rice made a great speech and I answered, the movie cameras following us all the time; handshakes all round, John nearly pulling Rice over in his excitement, Number Three "camera-stealing" like a Hollywood star, then we were in the car, and off.

With loud cheers ringing behind us, we rolled into St. James's Street, where I nearly ended the whole show by not seeing an approaching taxi.

Folkstone was to be our first stop, but with only another 9,985 miles between us and Capetown we had a puncture, which held us up so long that we missed our Channel boat, so we stayed the night in Surgeon Rear Admiral Parker's flat and were very gratified to see our pictures in all the evening papers.

The next day we were told that the car carrier had had an accident and would be late. The other two members said they were poor sailors, and preferred to travel on a boat that was at least whole, so they went ahead on the ordinary passenger ferry.

Later I ran the car on without trouble, but as soon as the carrier got under way the damage of the previous day was obvious; the mast or derrick under which the car was parked had been badly cracked, and every vibration of the engine threatened to bring it down.

# Chapter 2 ~ France

By the time the car was on shore at Boulogne the R. A. C. representative who was travelling on board had introduced me to the Customs officer and told him something of our proposed journey, so that when we walked down to the car he was much more interested in the question of whether we should get to the Cape than in whether we were smuggling.

Four hieroglyphics marked in chalk on the tyres indicated that we had complied with Customs formalities, and I was so pleased with this that I climbed into the back of the car over the piles of luggage and presented the officer with half a bottle of whisky. This seemed to surprise him, for he said, "Have you any more of this?" and when I said I had, he exclaimed, "*Mon Dieu, allez au Cap, vite!*" As my companions were just emerging from the harbour buffet after having their first cognac, we "allezed".

A bright sun cheered us on our way from Boulogne, although it was bitterly cold. To save expenses, I decided to try out our camping equipment, and twenty miles before the outskirts of Paris I found a cutting by the side of the road from which chalk was being quarried, which I thought would make an excellent windbreak.

To get out the few things we wanted seemed to necessitate the unpacking of the entire car, and soon the whole of the quarry was strewn with pieces of baggage. A stew was put on - and then it started to rain. In a few minutes we were lifting huge masses of mud and chalk on our feet at every step, while every package took its quota into the car. Then over went the stove, spreading the half-cooked stew among the rest of the goods, and we were now so cold and miserable that I ordered a tot of whisky for all hands and decided to push on for Paris.

It got colder and colder, which meant that my last order had to be repeated at most of the *estaminets* [French cafés] we passed, so perhaps it is not surprising that, having dropped the other two at a small hotel in Paris and driven off to garage the car, I could not remember the name of the hotel or the way back to it. At two a.m. I was still quartering Paris in a light fall of snow, but eventually found it.

At Fontainebleau it really started to snow, at Avallon it was worse, by Marcon it was impossible to see the sides of the road. At one point I had got off the main route and could see no guiding marks at all, so John and I got out to investigate. Suddenly, with a yell, he disappeared, and while I was peering round, trying to see what had happened, the Blue Train dashed past within a few yards. By the light of its windows we could see that we had climbed up the bank on an old road instead of following the main one, which dipped suddenly to tunnel under the railway line. John had slipped over the edge of the bank and was floundering and swearing in the snow below, and it took us over an hour to turn and get the car back onto the road proper again.

Taking it in turns to drive, with one to look out for signs and wipe the snow from the windscreen, and one asleep in the back, we pushed on. In the early hours of the morning we ran out of petrol just outside Villefranche, but were able to coast up to a petrol pump, coloured that inevitable blue which in France is spread impartially on shrines, petrol pumps, houses and advertisements. At least half an hour was spent in rousing the proprietor of the filling station, who finally emerged into the snow-covered street carrying a hurricane lamp, wearing only a nightshirt and a tasselled stocking cap and looking rather like Rip Van Winkle. I'm afraid neither of us was very polite to the other, but we got our petrol.

We were following the Rhone valley, where the turbulent river, swollen by the recent rains and snow, threatened at any moment to burst its banks.

The sun now came out and we all felt better. At one small town before Aix, we came into the square during a local agricultural show, and before we knew what had happened we were lined up in procession between a float representing the wine harvest and another which proclaimed in floral letters the encouraging news that someone or something had "milliards of francs to lend to the farmer".

At Marseilles we found that it would pay us to wait for the "Amazone", a ship belonging to one of the French lines, instead of taking a British boat. In the meantime we took a single unfurnished room in an evil-smelling house off the top of the Canebiere. Our camp beds were erected, and we lived on half-done food smoked on top of a double wicked oil-lamp and coffee and croissants purloined from the fly-blown bar below.

Still in pursuit of our economy campaign, we had elected to travel fourth class on the boat, so having got our Rolls parked safely on the main deck, we were led aft to where a seething mass of Zouaves [French soldiers], Arab pedlars and greasy-looking Jews were pouring down a hatchway into the bowels of the ship, which comprised the fourth class accommodation. Thanking our guide, we doubled on our tracks and took cover in the back of the car, emerging soon after we put to sea, to find the skipper and some of the Zouave officers examining the Rolls with interest. There was also a section of a Citroen desert exploration party on board with their specially built caterpillar track cars. Their personnel made somewhat discouraging remarks on our desert transport, but we pointed out that we were going much further than they were, and therefore had to consider other territory than desert. This gave us a topic of conversation, and we kept on happily explaining our route and drinking their bitter red wine, managing to head off any question of sending us below.

16

# Chapter 3 ~ Egypt

Little difficulty was experienced at Alexandria, although I had some nasty moments when the car was slung over the side and left dangling above a large bollard while the stevedores argued which way round it should land. The representatives of the oil company came down to meet us, so we had no trouble with the Customs.

During our stay in Alexandria the wheels and tyres were changed to give us a larger tyre area and prevent sinking in the desert sand, and the car was repainted with a dull silver sunproof paint, which made it look rather like the Queen of Sheba's State coach-cum-Capecart.

A certain amount of backlash had been noticeable in the diff., which the British armoured car unit offered to fix for us. Two sergeant mechanics came down, stripped the back axle, and reassembled it again, still with the backlash. A bottle of whisky and a bottle of gin were opened and went down their respective gullets, and I found their advice increasingly difficult to follow, while their injunction to, "Put a bit of sodder in the rad, Guv'nor" defeated me completely. It was only later that "sodder" was interpreted for me as soda.

The inspection of the rear axle had taken a few days, and I took the opportunity of renewing my acquaintance with this lovely port. I spent most of every day swimming with two Hungarian girls whom I found at the Pavilion Blu, and the evenings with an old friend of mine, Mr. Baker of the Pitsale Coal Company, with whom I went on a nightly round of the brighter spots. One of those evenings ended in an attempt to steal the sentry box from the grounds of the Royal Palace.

Several carloads of friends saw us off on the road to Cairo, and Baker accompanied us all the way there.

On arrival he introduced us to a number of people, including a Mr. Stewart Smith, who carried on his good work, so that we soon knew every bar and clubhouse in the place, I also brushed up my small knowledge of Arabic swear words, of which no language offers a better selection.

Before leaving, I decided to pay a lone visit to the Pyramids and the Sphinx to see if I could capture their romance in the rays of the full moon. Having got off the tram and fortified myself with a drink at the Mena House Hotel, I walked up the steep road that ascends to the plateau on which the Pyramids stand, and, with my shoes full of sand, reached a spot where I could gaze at the brooding eyes of the Sphinx. As I stared, the moon gradually rose, and I thought I could discern flitting shapes approaching. Behind me I heard the rustle of ghostly garments, then an insinuating voice:-

"You want dragoman [guide], Sah? Me very good dragoman, Sah!"

"No! Get the hell out of this!"

"Very good, Sah. Here my card... any time, Sah. Me good dragoman, Sah!"

Again peace; the shadows on the Sphinx's face had moved and it seemed to smile a little. I began to feel suitably awe-inspired, and then - several voices this time:-

"You want dragoman , Captain?"

"Me fine dragoman, Sah!"

"Me the original boy to run up Pyramid, Sah!"

"Oh, go to blazes!"

But the chant went on, new dragomen appearing, and finally I left. A sort of hallelujah chorus marched behind me, in spite of my dignified refusal even to see them, the effect of which was somewhat marred by one of my shoes coming off in the sand, whereupon they all sprang on it and returned it to me with great ceremony.

Having at last lost them, I decided to climb the smallest Pyramid and sat for a while on its top, at first gazing over the moonlit desert, but then, as I gradually got colder, looking more often the other way, where the lights of the hotel twinkled.

*[The Mena House Hotel, Cairo. (Present day)]*

It seemed there was no inspiration for me here and I had better return to my usual source, but on arrival at ground level I was arrested by a

18

policeman for climbing a Pyramid without a permit. However, the inevitable *baksheesh* [small bribe] put that right.

*The Rolls in Cairo*

In Cairo, we were notified that the Sudan Government absolutely refused to allow one vehicle to cross the desert alone. Nobody can be an explorer unless they are lucky, and I always was. I discovered almost immediately that a party of three Germans, calling themselves the *Deutsche Motorrad Afrika Expedition*, using three motor cycles and sidecars, was also in difficulties over the crossing, as the authorities did not think they could carry sufficient reserve supplies with them.

We made arrangements to travel in convoy, but they were to leave a day before us and we would catch them up. We travelled fast during the day, following the bank of the Nile, and threading our way through endless parties of donkeys, whose owners placidly sat on their rumps, some with flapping feet over their sterns or flanks, making small groups all facing each other, looking as if they only needed a spare donkey in the centre with a green baize rump to make a perfect poker party. They certainly weren't going to move for us, but luckily the donkeys had more sense and trotted into the ditch at the side, spilling their riders, to our huge satisfaction.

We kept going during the night, frequently held up by armed guards who spoke to us rapidly in Arabic, at the same time waving ancient and dangerous-looking rifles under our noses, but eventually letting us proceed without either side having understood the other.

Just as the sun started to show above the horizon, we came to our advance guard camped by the side of the Nile, with a savoury mess of pigeon soup simmering over a wood fire, and after a most satisfying meal we got going again. Sand stretched everywhere in a riot of variations of yellow and brown, broken occasionally by the mud-built houses and the palms that surrounded the many wells.

*The Heil Hitler lads join us*

At one spot we made a wonderful camp alongside irrigation canals of clear cold water; at another the ground was covered with the stubble of a garnered grain crop, and hardly had we got our tents erected, when the Arab farmer came to tell us that he was just going to irrigate the field, but later promised not to let the water in until after we had left in the morning. During the night I woke up and noticed a strong smell of burning, and on going outside found that a chain of smouldering fire was creeping towards us through the thrash. Having roused the camp, we all started stamping it out, but before we got it really down we saw that someone had opened the sluice and the water was pouring in. We only just managed to throw everything into the car and get back onto the road before we should have been bogged down.

Assiut, Sohag, Nag Hammadi and Dessara, with their bustling native life, were soon behind us, but before we reached Luxor we got our first check; a bridge over the confluence of two tributaries of the Nile was down, and the working party who were repairing it informed us that it would be two or three days before we could cross.

The road turned at a sharp angle across the bridge, while dead ahead of us was a large mound some hundred feet high, crowned with a mud-built fort. The mound sloped away to the river, which was fairly low, and after a little inspection I thought we might be able to ford it by taking a run at the mound and coming down on the other side.

The three motor cycles tried first, and with all the working gang pushing, got safely over. I then took the wheel of our three-ton car, and with a terrific roar charged the hill, but only got up some thirty feet. Backwards and forwards I charged, but could never quite get up. The car was then completely unloaded and ropes were attached to the front, and with all hands pulling and pushing we made the final ascent. Near the top, the right hand wheels left the ground, and it seemed that nothing could save the car and myself from rolling down into the river below, which would have been the end, not only of the expedition, but of me as well.

As the car started to tip, the Arabs fled with a yell, and I thought we were gone, but there was still sufficient forward movement for me to ram the radiator into and through the walls of the mud fort, where it stuck with huge chunks falling off the walls all round. It seemed that a post-mortem was about to be held, but I kept yelling "Push!" at the top of my voice, which they eventually did, until we went right through the fort, leaving its ruins behind us, and charged down the bank and up the other side.

When we came to collect our kit, we found that a great part of it was missing, and it took over half an hour beating up our previous helpers to get it back again. One hoary old rascal had our shovel down the back of his voluminous pants as his share of *baksheesh*.

Just before we left, the Arab foreman of the bridge gang came to me with a grubby piece of paper and a pencil, with the request "Pleese, Sir! You sign for the fort, pleese!"

At Luxor, the Vacuum Oil Company agent was all out to welcome us. He was the most excitable and hospitable Italian I have ever met. A long table was set under a shelter made from palm leaves, and he hastened to explain to me that as he did not know what we preferred to eat and drink he had got everything.

Opposite each man's seat was an array of bottles, whisky, gin, wine, sherry and varieties of beer, while huge platters contained fresh fish, fried, boiled, baked, different meats, and a huge bowl of the Arab dish known as cous-cous.

All the white people of Luxor were there, including the manager of the famous Luxor Hotel, who bewailed the fact the hotel was closed, but Horst, the leader of the German expedition, said we'd stay there anyway, and we did. With a super hotel to ourselves, we lived in style, bathing in the Nile from its steps and giving sumptuous parties on the proprietor's account.

From Luxor we experienced little difficulty in reaching Aswan, but from there to El Shellal we were in trouble. The only hard track through the soft yellow sand was that made by the railway, and with a fine disregard for the rights of things, I decided to take this route. All went well for a while, until we came to a construction camp, where the car stuck badly. An Australian miner who was in charge and whom I was to meet under curious circumstances later, came to our rescue, but instead of helping carted the others off for drinks, leaving me with a few natives to get the car going again.

The party re-formed in an hilarious state, and we bumped on over the sleepers, but not for long; again we stuck, the car in front and the three motor cycles behind. After half an hour's solid pushing and digging we had not moved more than three feet, when we heard the distant shrill whistle of an approaching train.

Redoubled efforts got us perhaps another six inches, and by that time the shriek of brakes heralded the arrival of the express. As soon as it stopped, excited officials and passengers debouched from both sides and descended on us.

The Arab guard outdid himself in every language I had ever heard of and several I had not, and ended up with, "You stoppa da train I t'row da dam' t'ing off da line; I spit!"

Having worked for over an hour in the terrific rays of the sun, I was not at my best and did not give the answer that turneth away wrath, but told all and sundry that if they could chuck it off the damned line, I couldn't. The whole train crew and most of the passengers got to work, and we were soon at the bottom of the bank. In the meantime the Germans had wheeled their motor cycles off, and were strolling about with the attitude of "no connection with the firm next door."

With a last derisive toot, the express got under way, the guard hanging out behind breathing threats of what he and the company would do when they made connection with the Nile steamer and returned.

Having found our bearings, I discovered that the sand here was quite hard, and we struggled on to El Shellal, arriving late at night. The train was at the siding and the passengers on board. We crept in as quietly as possible, and having found what I thought was an unoccupied compartment, we strewed our kit round and prepared to turn in. Before we could get down to it, who should turn up but the guard. With one wild shriek he was off again. It was no good trying to cope with him on his own ground, so we got out the gramophone and put on a record in Arabic. What it was I don't know, but he stopped his tirade to listen for a moment, and before he could get going again I placed half a glass of whisky in his hand, and every time he looked like starting again we filled his glass, eventually parking him outside the door and sleeping comfortably in his quarters.

Daylight presented us with more problems; first the guard, with a very sore head, and then the news that the Nile steamer could not accommodate our car, and that we should have to wait some ten days while they fetched a barge for us.

However, most of these days we spent very pleasantly, chiefly swimming from the half-submerged temple of Isis at Philae, diving from the top of its walls and coming up through the entrances to admire the painted frescoes, which still retained a great deal of their thousands-of-years-old colour.

At last our barge arrived, and we found that instead of going up with the regular service, we were to be lashed alongside an old paddle-wheel boat that was carrying cargo, and to make matters worse the mail train came in again and we discovered that the skipper was a friend of the guard's.

The night before we left, we had a terrific party on board the Nile boat that met the train, which reached its climax when Horst and I dived from the top deck into the Nile in an alleged attempt to catch crocodiles, then came ashore, and taking the sidecar off one of the motor cycles, had the wildest ride I have ever had along the railway behind the train, with our old friend the guard waving and yelling imprecations at us from the last carriage while the passengers cheered us on.

# Chapter 4 ~ Sudan

The boat was to take us to Wadi Halfa. This was a particularly bad stretch of sand and we knew we had to get through fairly quickly, for rains to the south were due, and if they started to fall, we should be blocked. We rather wished we had risked it, as our first day on the iron decks were like being on the top of a stove, while at night the river mosquitoes, of which there are none worse in the world, descended on us in millions. To add to this, the skipper would not allow us off the barge, being very peeved with us, especially after Horst had lost the ship's best bucket, throwing it over the side to draw up water, under the impression that he had tied a rope to it, and as we expected to travel with the ordinary passenger boat, we had practically no food on board.

Horst decided to take one of his machines down, and worked stripped to the waist, getting so sunburnt in the process that he could not move for days afterwards.

Slowly we chugged our way up river, passing some marvellous figures cut in the rock on the bank. Once, five fully-grown elephants watched our progress from the river's edge. Every now and again we stuck on some sandbank or snag, and had to be pushed off with long poles by the crew. One night a school of hippopotamus followed us, their backs gleaming in the spotlights we shone on them.

At last Wadi Halfa showed round the bend of the river, and we were soon ashore, where we were met by the officials of the Sudan Railway, who put us up for the night and gave us really valuable information regarding our route.

When we went for our petrol supplies, the Vacuum Oil Company agent proved to be a fine old Arab, some six feet tall, with a flowing red beard, a dark green robe worked with gold designs, and a round hat with a gold top and a pink turban wound round it. He was in a foul temper, having had his place burnt down the day before, which was hardly our fault.

The desert proper started as soon as we left Wadi Halfa, and we arranged that Horst should lead, followed by Beppo, the youngest of the German party, then Heinz, who was the oldest of us all and, having spent some years in Tanganyika, rather looked down on us as mere boys, and then came our outfit.

I had stipulated that I should be in sole charge of the convoy, as there can only be one leader on a job like this. The day's orders were that we should travel in this way to see how it worked, that we should not lose

24

sight of each other, and that after each half hour Horst would stop and we should close up to confer. However, the motor cycles proved to be too fast for us; we lost sight of them and could only keep check on them by watching their tracks in the sand. I saw that one machine had gone straight on, while the other two had gone to the west of a large sand dune. We stopped, and after about three-quarters of an hour Horst came back to us without having seen them.

Our car was parked on a fairly high spot, and with myself on the carrier of the motor cycle, we set off to find the strays. Within half a mile we found Heinz, sitting on the side of the sand dune with a large coloured golf umbrella fixed to the handlebars of his machine; he was trying, without much success, to mend a puncture, the tools getting so hot in the sun that he couldn't hold them. There was no sign of Beppo, so we told Heinz to wait and followed up the tracks.

Later the sand got softer, the tracks fading out under the caress of the wind, and we lost them. I attempted to climb a dune, but having taken a run up it found it soft and loose, rather like quicksand, and had to throw myself down and roll back to firm ground again. However, I had had time to see a speck in the distance, which proved to be our truant; he was sitting calmly there, waiting for us to pick him up, with no idea that he was off the track.

We collected Heinz on the way back to the car, having wasted nearly two hours.

One of the landmarks for which we were looking was a slatey outcrop of rock round which a curious legend centres. It is said that tracks never vanish from the sand in its lee, which has a peculiar coarse surface studded with a mosaic of small pebbles, and that the tracks of General Gordon's guns are still to be seen here. We certainly found hundreds of tracks looking as fresh as if they had been made the year before, and I spent a few moments drawing the League badge, which may remain there until the end of time, rain being practically unknown here.

Actually the railway ran across this Nubian Desert stretch, but we found that owing to soft sand, we had to keep far to the east of the line, where there was harder going and we could seldom keep it in sight. There were ten stations or halts, at each of which we had to report our safe arrival to the Arab in charge, who would produce the ceremonial cup of camomile tea and afterwards some excellent coffee, served in crude but beautiful earthenware cups.

The sand was becoming softer and softer, and the motor cycles were in continual trouble and had to be dug out time after time; gruelling work in a temperature of over 100°F [37°C], while all hands had to push each vehicle into the small town of Abu Hamard.

From here we struck out onto the undulating surface of the desert and were soon swallowed up in its vastness, travelling entirely by compass. As each machine crested a rise it was visible for a few moments and was then lost to view in a hollow, but we were all keeping close together, with myself sitting on our cab roof keeping the direction, while Horst prospected ahead for the firmest route. This worked excellently, and we made our next point a small place called Abu Dis.

The going then got steadily worse, and I had to spell either Beppo or Heinz on their motor cycles, and also take a hand at breaking the track for Horst. Forty miles a day was good going, but tempers were getting badly frayed. The other two had definitely formed an Anti-Filby Society, while Heinz was proving troublesome in the other camp, and it was with a sigh of relief that I picked up the outlines of some jagged hills, a landmark for which we were looking. From these hills we had to take a course due west to strike the Nile, but although we pushed forward day after day we could not pick it up, and we came to the conclusion that our compass had gone wrong. A test at night by the stars proved this to be so, and a change in direction eventually got us there.

We reached what was to have been one of our petrol dumps, but the ancient Arab guardian told me that no petrol had arrived for me - however, he could sell me some at 16/- per gallon. It was, according to him, a super petrol, called "Capnfilly" petrol. We had to have some, so I told him to haul it out, and was overjoyed to find that the "Capnfilly" was "Captain Filby" stamped on each case, and that it was really our supply.

We also managed to purchase some very woolly-looking potatoes and some very hard but excellent dates, and, much to my surprise, some tins of pineapple, tinned by Tan Kah Kee, an old friend of mine in Singapore.

We were now on the river again, and I managed to shoot three ducks, two of which we lost, the current washing them away before we could get to them.

The sand was still very soft, and we had been particularly warned against a spot know as the Wadi Amur, which, when we came to it, I judged to be a prehistoric river bed, now full of soft wind-blown sand.

Camping for a while, Horst and I prospected up and down it, and eventually found what appeared to be a good crossing. Tempers were running high at what was thought by the others to be a waste of time, and Heinz started up his motor cycle and attempted to cross straight ahead. For a while we saw him mounting the crests of sand, and then he disappeared, and with the engines roaring out and in low gear we just got across with an occasional push from everybody. This had taken some time, but when we arrived down the other bank at the point opposite where Heinz had vanished, there was still no sign of him, nor were there any tracks on this side.

Horst and I set off on foot to find him and soon picked up his gay coloured umbrella in one of the hollows. The machine lay on its side in a hole with Heinz stretched beside it. In a desperate effort to get across before we did, he had torn off his shirt and had started digging with his hands, only to have the motor cycle slip in on him. The sun had got to work and he was stretched out and half buried, and there is little doubt that another half hour would have seen the end of him.

We carried him back and put him under the car, the only shade to be found in that burnished, simmering expanse, our thermometer showing that the temperature in the cab of the car was 139°F [59.4°C].

His motor cycle was pulled out and Heinz was put in the back of the car while I mounted his machine and took the lead for the rest of the day. A headwind blew in our faces like the blast from a furnace door, and it was impossible to breathe unless we tied handkerchiefs across our noses and mouths.

The next day the sand was much firmer, and we were able to increase our speed, but the undulations were becoming much more abrupt, and many times we were almost over. Then we were in soft sand again, which meant manhandling once more. Finally we got to a small deserted oasis, where most of the party collapsed and had to have water brought to them. Horst and I seemed to be standing things much better than the rest, with the possible exception of Beppo.

For over an hour we cast ahead trying to find a firm patch that we could cross, and at last found a tongue that was just wide enough to carry the car. Shimmering mirages on either hand distracted the eye from following the course we had marked, and if even one wheel slipped off it meant half an hour's hard work to get it going again.

Heinz was once more in trouble; travelling too fast, his motor cycle turned over, pinning him to the ground, and as the engine was racing there seemed to be every possibility that it would catch fire. As we were on a particularly soft patch we had to keep the car moving and could not stop to help him. I saw his friends racing back towards him; however, as soon as they got close they set up a movie camera and started to film the spill, with Heinz still pinned under the motor cycle, swearing in German.

Every way we looked appeared to be exactly the same, the small smooth hillocks of sand rolling away to the horizon giving the impression of a heavy swell at sea. A shout from the leader and his wildly flourishing arms indicated that something exceptional was ahead, and I dreaded what I should find, as we were getting played out. Each machine as it got to the rise stopped, and I could see that Heinz and Beppo were stripping.

Mystified, we pushed on as fast as possible, to find that we were on the banks of the Nile, and by the time we caught up with them, the Germans were already wallowing in its brown but life-giving waters. This vast river could not be seen even from fifty yards away. I soon joined them, but my confreres refused to come in, alleging that there were crocs all along the river. This caused the first real break, as I completely lost my temper and offered to throw them in. They both took a determined stand, so I eventually cooled off and went back to wallow, knowing that it would put me absolutely right for the next stretch.

Following the river bank as far as possible, we came at last to the town of Sherika and took up our quarters in the resthouse. Before we could get settled in, the native headman rode up with a request from the District Commissioner that we should join him.

Still covered in fine powdery sand and with parched throats, we followed our guide through the busy market place, edging our way between vendors who sat on the ground displaying their merchandise - dates, bolts of cloth, cigarettes, the bloody carcass of a goat, and a hundred and one other wares, and eventually coming to a well-built whitewashed house, where our host stood on the cool porch ready to welcome us.

Almost his first words were "Beer or whisky?" and a pint of deliciously cold beer slid over our tongues, to be followed by a sparkling glass of whisky and soda *with ice* floating on top.

We now felt strong enough to introduce ourselves formally, the Germans clicking their heels, shooting out their hands, and ejaculating "Horst Millauer", "Heinz Dingler", "Ernst Mielke" in turn, to which I refrained from adding "And Uncle Tom Cobley and all".

*Herr Dingler*

Hardly had these formalities been concluded, when a smartly dressed native servant appeared to announce that a bath was ready.

An excellent dinner was served, at which we were introduced to ground-nut soup for the first time, the gramophone was put on, and then, with the pipes going, we lolled back in comfort.

Beds had been prepared for us on the flat-topped roof, and we were soon in them, my last waking consciousness registering the long-drawn-out call of "Allah il Allah" from the mosque.

It seemed that I had hardly dozed off before I again heard the call of the *muezzin* which welcomed the dawn and summoned all good Mussulmen to prayer.

As if it had been a signal, our host's two dogs leapt on my bed and started to lick my face; there followed a scamper round the roof top with them, which led over the beds of the other sleepers, and we were told that ponies were at the door if we wished to ride.

Our Number Three, he of the Guardsman's moustache [Teddy], and myself set off at a canter down the dirty main street, scattering donkeys and camels on all sides, then back for a bath and a wonderful breakfast.

The sun was now well on its journey, and we had to be on ours. We refused "one for the road", made our *adieux*, and had a practically trouble-free run to Atbara.

Here we were again hospitably entertained, and, what was even more pleasant, found that we were back among vegetation once more. It was here that we first saw the curious loofah tree. I had always thought that the familiar long accessory to a bath was of the sponge family, and was surprised to see them hanging on long stems of quite large trees, looking rather as if they had been attached like presents on a Christmas tree.

# Chapter 5 ~ Sudan

The Germans' motor cycles had suffered badly, the route over which we had come being plainly marked by pieces of their outfit which had either been jettisoned or had fallen off, so they decided that from here, they would continue by train and river boat, and we said farewell to them.

Crossing the Nile on a crazy-looking pontoon, we followed a fair track which wound among low, stunted growth, all of which was protected by wicked needle-like thorns, some of them over three inches long. After El Damer this faded out and thousands of camel tracks led in every direction with no indication of which was the one we should follow.

An extraordinarily pretty gorge looked inviting, and we wended our way through it, dodging huge varicoloured rocks, in the welcome shade of the palms, which here were plentiful. Once more into open country, where we had to admit we were lost. Our compass got us back to the banks of the Nile, where we were able to see a fair track on the other side, but there was no means of crossing, which necessitated our making our own track to Shendi.

We had lunch at Shendi with the officers of the British regiment stationed there, coming in for a good deal of chaff at having lost our way. They were very interested in our expedition, and seemed to consider that if we got through safely it was more than possible we should be given a new car. One of them, however, thought this was extremely doubtful, citing an experience of his own. It seemed that during the war he had marched many thousands of miles, always wearing a pair of boots made by a well-known British manufacturer. He had brought them home, and having written an interesting account of their travels, had taken them to the manufacturers, confident that he would get a fat cheque and a new pair of boots when they saw what wonderful value his old ones would be to their advertising campaign. But on presenting himself, and his screed having been read, he was asked what his complaint was, as the boots seemed to have done all that the makers had claimed for them, and they did not feel responsible for the fact that they were now worn out.

We were still on the wrong side of the Nile, and had great difficulty in finding our way through the ugly thorn bushes that did not boast a leaf between them, yet managed to obscure any clear view of what lay ahead. Later, however, we picked up the railway line again, and camped at one of the small stations.

During the night I woke to hear what I thought was a hyena prowling round the camp. Leaning out of bed, I grasped a fair sized stone and heaved it in the direction of the noise. Unfortunately it landed on a sleeping Arab, who woke with a yell and accused the man sleeping next to him of throwing it. Soon the whole camp were shouting at each other, and I informed my partners, who were now sitting up, that I thought there was an Arab rising, which didn't cheer them up much. I then dropped off to sleep again.

Before we got away in the morning, a wire which had been sent to all stations was handed to me, saying that plague had broken out and that under no circumstances were we to stop, but to report to Khartoum immediately. Luckily we had picked up a fair track, but the wind was increasing, and we were getting into the sand area again. By two o'clock it was blowing half a gale, and the flying sand made it impossible to see more than ten yards.

Then down went our wheels again, and we had to start digging ourselves out, the wind blowing the sand back into the hole again almost as fast as it was lifted out. We were now getting close to Omdurman, the great mud city that was the Mhadi's capital, so we were not particularly surprised to see a number of goatherds turn up. These were pressed into service and helped us with our digging.

One of them elected to guide us to the city, the track to which led through some curious hills composed of huge blocks of stone piled on each other in fantastic disorder as if giant children had been playing with them.

With the wind and sand still shrieking past us, we at last made the fine bridge spanning the Nile and were soon unloading at the Grand Hotel.

I always wake at dawn, and the following morning I was astonished to hear the roaring of lions. I had no idea they came so far north, and full of excitement I leapt out of bed and rushed in to call the others, waking them madly and telling them to grab the cameras while I got hold of a native who would lead us to them. They didn't seem keen, but nevertheless started hurriedly to dress, while the roars echoed through the hotel.

I dashed downstairs and found an Arab and asked him if he could guide us to where we could best get photos of the King of Beasts who dared come right up to the town. He replied, "You no want guide, Sah. The zoo is just ovah there." John, arriving with cameras slung round him, was distinctly annoyed, and accused me of another dam' fool joke to get them out of bed early, so I let it go at that.

We were made honorary members of the beautiful club in Khartoum, and had a very enjoyable break. During the day, the Germans arrived by train and joined us. They intended staying for a while and then taking the river boat again.

From Khartoum we took a guide who brought us over very fair tracks to Wad Medani. At 2 am. the mail train came through, and we went down to the station and bought extra provisions from the restaurant car, in company with the rest of the townspeople, mostly Italians, to whom the arrival of the train was an event.

We were now among an intricate system of canals, and - for a wonder - our Teddy was driving, and nearly put us into a canal. We were now making excellent progress, rattling through small villages deserted except for goats and donkeys, which rolled and kicked in the road, throwing up clouds of dust that shone pink in the dawning light.

Stopping to cook breakfast, I had my jacket stolen, its pockets containing my passport, pipe, watch, and a considerable sum of money. We could find no trace of it, and we could not stop for long, as we always had that bugbear of the rains hanging over us.

At Makwar I reported the loss to the District Commissioner, and though he immediately sent out police to interrogate the villagers on our route, I never saw it again.

After a short stay, during which we all shared a bath, due to a water shortage, we were off once more. Presently we came to a large village that was exactly like a maze; the streets were hedged by screens of bamboo matting, the lanes between all looking exactly alike. Whichever way we turned we always came back again to the same spot. Night had fallen, and as we roared up one lane, down the next, and up another, we woke the whole town, who gathered at the point at which we kept repeatedly turning up. Eventually the headman came to our rescue and produced a guide, who was to take us to the next village.

That man certainly had a flattering idea of the capabilities of our car, for he took us in a direct line over ploughed fields and dykes, through scattered houses where the villagers, sleeping outside in the warm night, sat up and watched us pass in amazement. I should not have liked to do our guide's return journey on foot in the darkness, as we had seen many eyes gleaming in the light of our headlamps, but he set off quite happily.

A fine-looking bridge, carrying the railway and the road, crossed the White Nile at Kosti, and I was blissfully in ignorance of the fact that we had to have a special pass permitting us to cross, and even with that, were not supposed to cross at night.

When the car was on the bridge, we found that we had exactly two inches either side to spare, and it was nervy work steering, with the moon making a silvery path on the river far below us. I hung out of the driving seat and we cautiously proceeded, the others hanging out the other side and telling me to keep well over, but you can't do much with only four inches to play with.

We were almost across when, with a yell, a sentry rose, apparently from under our bonnet, and stood with his bayonet practically touching our radiator.

My Arabic was not good enough to cope with the situation, and we seemed to have reached an impasse, as we certainly could not go back and he didn't appear inclined to let us come on. His shouts produced the rest of the guard, which did not help matters, and finally I climbed along the side of the car, John taking my place, while our Number Three sat up in state and made great play with his moustache. I then pointed dramatically to our Union Jack flying on the front wing, stood to attention, and saluted the occupants of the car. It worked. The guard sprang to attention, presented arms, and we were through. I often wonder who he said we were in his morning report.

It was still heavy going, but the track was well marked. We were getting desperately tired, and, needless to say, bad-tempered. Never again will I have three on an expedition, as two will always get together to oppose the third, and it's the small things on a trip like this that can be so exasperating, such as Teddy's habit of spending valuable time in the morning carefully combing his moustache and, believe it or not, putting on a moustache trainer, when we wanted to get underway while the sand was still firm after the cool of the night.

Late in the afternoon we came on some tents, and were greeted with a shout in broadest Scotch of, "Hi, mon, but ye're wearing an Ayrshire number!" Frankly, I had no idea where our number plate had come from. To me it was simply a number, and as far as I knew the car was not registered in any part of the world, but I agreed pleasantly that this was so, and, knowing Scotland rather well, we were soon swapping reminiscences over the liquid for which that country is famous. However, we three were so tired that we kept dropping off to sleep, eventually curling up for a few hours, to be wakened by our new-found friend and given a meal before starting.

Black soil, cracked into huge fissures by the heat, threatened to shake the car to pieces, then more sand, and the amazing sight of a sand dune some hundred and fifty feet high, coloured blood-red in the setting sun, which looked as if it would be impassable until we found that two cement tracks had been laid over it, which carried us into Rahad.

Before we arrived at the District Commissioner's house, we came on a native policeman making traffic signs, and our attempts to obey these put the car off the track, where it stuck firmly. Walking ahead, I introduced myself to the District Commissioner, who asked us to stop the night with him, an invitation we accepted with pleasure. He then opened up the prison, and a large gang of prisoners soon had the car back on the tracks again.

During a pleasant meal our host gave us some idea of the vastness of the area which he controlled and the nature of his work. At the moment he was particularly troubled over the question of water rights, especially among the owners of huge bullock herds, who had a constant feud with those who owned camels. He mentioned, without any particular stress, that there was a ghost inhabiting this area which left tracks that changed from those of a man to those of a camel and then again to those of a goat. I didn't like to press the matter, though I would have given much to know whether the story, as he told it, was his own firm conviction, as it seemed to be, or whether he was merely retelling a native yarn.

We slept that night in the open, inside huge cages made of mosquito-proof netting. Up at dawn I accompanied our host to the river, where literally thousands of bullocks, camels and goats were coming down to drink.

We got away in the cool of early morning, and an excellent road took us to El Obeid, the local headman meeting us some miles before we got there and escorting us to his house. Here we had really excellent coffee and were provided with a meal composed of what looked and tasted like a coarse sand-impregnated blanket on which reposed hard-boiled eggs and greasy chunks of what was probably goat, cooked in oil. Having conveyed to the others that the old chap would probably be frightfully offended if this was not eaten, I persuaded my host to take me out to the kitchen and show me how this really super coffee was made, and he conducted me to another room, leaving the others stuffing down the poisonous-looking meal. A boy produced half a gourd filled with red-hot charcoal, into which the coffee beans were poured, and then the whole contents were tossed over and over until the coffee was roasted, giving out a glorious smell. The beans were then separated and crushed, and it was ready to make.

The meal having disappeared (I found later the other two had most of it in their pockets) a move was made to the Government resthouse, where an invitation awaited us to dine with the Provincial Governor, and no sooner had we washed and changed then some of the transport fellows appeared and carted us off to their mess, where we had a very cheery time.

With only a few minutes to spare, we turned up at our dinner appointment. The Governor proved a most entertaining host, but his Assistant District Commissioner hinted to me that we were not really correctly dressed for such a function. Whether he thought we should carry evening kit on such a trip I didn't learn.

To bed very late, and up to find ponies waiting to take us for a quick gallop before breakfast, then off once more, only to come to grief in the soft sand. This caused us some hours' delay while we completely unloaded the car, having to cut what we took to be marshmallows to pack under the wheels, beastly things that oozed a thick, sticky, milky sap all over everything.

The everlasting monotony of the yellow sand, and the inevitable dress of the inhabitants, which looked like dirty sheets, had been so consistent since we left Cairo that it became an accepted fact, but we were now getting into more interesting country, the Nubian Mountains. Here the track wound its way among the foothills, vegetation was becoming more plentiful and was actually green, and it was here that we struck the huge trees that were used as containers for water. Some sixty feet in circumference, the trunks were hollow. Whether this was natural I never learnt. It seemed that each tree was the private property of some family who would fight to the death for its preservation, and age-old feuds centred round nearly all of them.

*[The baobab can contain 30,000 gallons of water.]*

I don't know if explorers are supposed to know all the languages of the parts through which they pass. It seems to me they must, as they always come back with such detailed accounts of the natives and their customs. For my part I usually depended on sign language, which worked quite well if you wanted a drink or something simple like that, but rather failed when you wanted to ask a native what tribe he belonged to. I should therefore hesitate to say that the tall strong men and women we were meeting were Nubians, though when I asked them they said "Um" and grinned. Of course if I had been the first white man here I should have called them Ums and everyone would have been satisfied.

They were wild-looking people, practically unclothed, while in some cases the men had their bodies painted all over, with their hair done up in little knobs with what looked like flour. By sign language I enquired the reason for these decorations, and the answer was "Um" and a grin, but later they went through the motions of throwing their spears, walking as if tired, and then pulling off a knob of the floury-looking stuff and eating it. I gathered that they were going on a long ceremonial hunt and that the flour knobs would provide emergency rations. They also had a peculiar habit of resting one foot on the other knee and standing for ages like storks.

35

Many of them had their hair coloured a bright red, which somehow looked incongruous against their black skins. Their weapons consisted of long spears, bows and arrows, and they carried serviceable-looking clubs. As we approached they would cluster together with the men in front as though they expected to be attacked; however, they were soon swarming around the car, looking at themselves in the driving mirror and all talking furiously.

There was great competition for the coloured matchsticks we were using, which they picked up and stuck in holes in their ears for ornaments, while the present of the top of a tobacco tin lid with a piece of string threaded through it to make a pendant to a necklace was so highly appreciated by one of the local dignitaries that he hurried off and presently reappeared with six women. I'm not sure whether he intended to offer them to me as wives or merely as a working party.

*A handsome pair of Negroes*

We were still travelling at night and passed through two small villages in the dark, daylight finding us well into the mountains where the native villages were perched high up among the rocks, so that they could easily be defended against the slave raiders who came across the Abyssinian [Ethiopian] border.

During a short camp, a party of what we took to be Abyssinians wended their way down the mountain side towards us, fine-looking

36

fellows with small goatee beards, riding stocky bullocks and all armed with terrifically long spears.

As they got to the camp the leader dismounted, and when I approached, they each solemnly shook hands, their palms feeling like very rough hard leather. They probably took us for Government officials, and were trying to impress on us that they had no slaves; or perhaps a slave train was being hurried away over the hills while they held us in dignified but unintelligible conversation. Eventually they rode off, and we continued our journey.

We were still on quite a good track. Rivers, dry at the time, were crossed by fords, many of the small bridges having been broken down by wild elephants. These fords seemed to be locally known as "Irish bridges", and were in some cases made of concrete. Designed and built by the Assistant District Commissioners, who seemed to be jacks-of-all-trades, some of the bridges were actually not negotiable, and we preferred to use the river bed itself.

# Chapter 6 ~ Sudan

Before reaching Tonga and rejoining the Nile, the route began to get very muddy, and at one point the track had to be left and the car pulled through the scrub by means of pulleys and ropes, using five purchases. The rate of travel could never have been more than an inch a minute, so that it often took us hours at a stretch, wallowing in mud, to cross some bad depression where the water lay.

Later, the track improved until we reached the French missionary station, where two Fathers worked, one of whom had been out from France for nearly forty years. He informed us that the other had been home quite recently, only twenty-eight years ago.

Here we made the curious discovery of two Foden steam wagons rusting on the banks of the Nile. How they got there or what they were for, Heaven knows; they could certainly never have been used on the soft earth roads in this country.

We now turned directly northward again, following the river bank as we should have to cross the Nile at Malakal. Here we ran into our first swarm of locusts. We could see them at first coming in huge clouds from the west, and I pointed them out to my confreres as mosquitoes. The missionaries, who were accompanying us for a short distance, played up beautifully and assured my friends that they were indeed mosquitoes, and that they had to climb into the boilers of the Fodens for protection when they got really bad.

The last part of the journey was on a tongue of land raised above the slimy mud of the Sudd that only just carried the car.

Malakal, the other side of the river, looked a very pleasant spot, with its red-roofed houses smothered in purple bougainvillea, but we couldn't attract anyone's attention as we perched on our hill surrounded by mud.

At last a native came over with a canoe made by burning and chipping out a tree-trunk, and in this crazy contraption, which threatened to turn turtle at any moment and deposit me in the swift current among the crocodiles, I crossed to the other side.

I visited the first house I came to, and after the rites of a drink had been complied with, was taken to the Governor's office. He issued instructions for the Government boat to bring us across, which it did after some anxious moments of manoeuvring to get the car from the bank on board and then off on the other side.

It was still early in the morning, so we did very full justice to the super breakfast that we had with the Governor. It seemed at first that we were not allowed to proceed, as we might easily get lost, there being no regular track, and the natives of the district were particularly wild and savage. However, after a lot of persuasion, we at last got his consent to push on, but only on condition that we carried six weeks' provisions.

From here it became a nightmare dash to get through before the rains made further progress impossible. The tracks, such as they were, were made up by piling earth high in the centre, just before the rains, so that they would be washed down level when the rains came, and to make matters worse they were composed of cracked cotton soil, so that we dropped into a fissure every two feet, and moreover had to travel at a precarious angle with two wheels on the top of the bank and the others in the trough.

Sunset saw us crossing the Sobat River on a crazy-looking ferry propelled by natives who kept their long spears beside them as they paddled. As we crossed, the leader, who was the only one wearing any clothes at all, produced a piece of paper from his rags and presented it to us. It was a demand by an Assistant District Commissioner that so much should be paid on presentation for work done by his village, and it was with great difficulty that we explained to him we were not Government officials.

After a few hours' sleep, we woke to find that a fine drizzle of rain was falling, and already the surface of the road was going. The wheels were soon clogged with mud. Chains when fitted only made things worse, while to step out of the car was to pick up a huge clod of mud on each foot.

We laboured on, knowing that if we stopped, we stopped for three months at the least if the rains really caught us, then the U-bolt on the back spring snapped, letting the body down on the wheels, and we started struggling and cursing to get it raised so that we could fix it.

I lay in the mud on my back and braced my legs against the body, raising it with the aid of jacks so the others could get boxes wedged under it. Then one of the front spring U-bolts was taken off and fixed on the back.

A few yards further, and down into the mud we would go again, the wheels spinning and throwing out great clods behind. Each time we went down John would say, "Now we are bitched", while our Number Three would flop hopelessly round in the mud, but by this time I had the bit between my teeth and with vile insults I urged them on for another few yards until we reached a sheet of water that was obviously impossible to cross without help.

We were now only a short distance from Kongor. Splashing and sliding through the water and the mud I made the town and got a large party of natives together, who got us out and towed us into the village. We were so tired that we crawled into one of the huts, muddy and filthy as we were, and slept.

As soon as it was light we were on the move again. It had stopped raining, but we could see the heavy clouds advancing from the north. There was a repetition of the previous day's performance, and at one place I had to fell a large tree to act as a lever to get us out of a bad patch.

Fortunately there were many natives about, who were only too willing to help in exchange for a small present of tobacco. These were Dinkas, the men being some of the tallest I have seen in Africa, while the women were fine-looking specimens of humanity.

After any particularly tough spot we would rest for a while, which meant that my pipe was immediately lighted, and I became the hub of a circle of absolutely nude women, who solemnly took their pipes from their mouths when I did or blew out smoke when I did.

At night we were almost driven mad by the mosquitoes which descended on us in swarms, the high-pitched metallic buzz of their wings playing treble to the bass of thousands of frogs who opened up a nightly chorus.

We had only just managed to get to a place called Bor, passing a large herd of elephants on the way, when a terrific storm broke, compelling us to spend that day and the next night there as the guest of the District Commissioner. I'm afraid we were poor company, as we slept most of the time, while I know I was frightfully irritable and rather disgraced myself in an argument on Christian Science, in which our host believed, so that when we left the other two had all his sympathy.

Just as we were going, a missionary from further down the river came in to say the road was practically under water but we might get through, and asked for a lift to his mission.

We moved forward in a series of short rushes from one fairly dry point to the next, backing to get up sufficient speed for each dash. John was driving and doing well. The windscreen was thickly smothered in mud, so I hung out on the running board giving him warning of tree-stumps and potholes, and each time we went into the muddy pools I was covered from head to foot in dripping slime.

Backing up a slight rise in preparation for the next dash, the gear lever was put into first, the engine roared up, the clutch was let in, but we did not move. At last something had given out.

There were so many mosquitoes hurrying towards us as it grew dark that we could hardly see out of bitten and swollen faces, and we had to abandon the car and plunge forward in the mud to the mission station, with the grunting of hippo in the river at our side and the noise of a leopard hurrying our progress.

The following morning John and I returned to the car with a party of natives, and after taking the body off, pushed the chassis to the highest point we could find, as we expected floods, and there stripped the rear axle, to find that the half shaft had snapped off short.

Having written a message to the makers in London asking for a spare, Teddy returned to Bor to have it wired home.

John and I spent several days hiding in the body of the car under mosquito nets during showers and dismantling the axle in readiness for the spare if it should ever get to us.

The natives, who were, I think, Newls, squatted round us in a circle, following every movement with their eyes. Early every morning they would arrive from their village, which was composed of very large communal huts, in which not only they, but their cattle passed the night. Fires were kept burning in these, and they would smother themselves with wood ash to keep off the mosquitoes. Their morning ablutions consisted merely of rubbing the worst of the ash out of their eyes, with the result that they arrived as grey-white natives with two black circles for eyes.

They also kept a good fire going for us in the camp, and into this I threw the non-skid tyre chains, and when they were red hot, grilled on them the fish they used to bring us, still wriggling from the river. Never have I tasted anything better.

In the evenings, the natives would throw green leaves on the fire and sit in the smoke as an added mosquito protection, while we sat under dripping nets and conversed by sign language. One huge fellow, whose sole clothing consisted of a bronze and copper armlet, attached himself to me; if my pipe went out he would pick up a live ember from the fire with his bare hands, or would turn over my fish with the blade of his spear.

Others brought weird white bulbous-looking roots which we ate raw with a tin of sardines, giving the tin and some of the oil, with which they smeared their bodies.

Just before dark they would go bounding off to their village, shouting and hollering to each other to scare off leopard, which were plentiful. John hit on an ingenious scheme to keep these beasts away from us. He would balance all our cooking and petrol tins in a circle round the camp connected by our tow rope, the idea being that if a leopard approached, it would knock the whole show over and the noise of falling tins would scare it. He would then go off into a sleep from which nothing short of an earthquake would wake him, and the tins would overbalance, nearly frightening the life out of me with the noise.

I decided we must get to the mission, so on went the wheels, then the body, and the tow ropes were tied on in front. About forty natives were eventually induced to hold onto these, but they only roared with laughter when I made signs that they should pull.

Finally, by taking the lead myself, with John steering, I got the idea into their heads, and they entered into the spirit of the thing. Leading at a fast run, followed by the whole party, who roared at the top of their voices, I charged through the mud, leaping over stumps, at which the noise

41

redoubled, the huge silver car bumping behind with John also yelling at the top of his voice. We did that five miles in record time.

The women were carrying the men's spears, and rushed madly round and round the runners, making a shrill warbling noise with their tongues between their lips, so that we must have looked like a triumphal procession of the ancient kings.

The missionary arranged payment for their labour, although I think they would have done it for nothing, as we had become firm friends. However, he demanded that they should be paid, so it was done in *tarifas*, a small coin with a hole in it worth a quarter of a *piastre*, the whole bill coming to less than ten shillings.

That night we stayed at the mission and had an insight into the mentality of this European who was bringing a civilised outlook to the lives of the natives. On his verandah was a large sugar box in which were a number of young crocodiles. I asked him if he was keeping them as pets, but he said no, they had been given to him and they were far too dangerous to be liberated; it was against his principles to kill them, but, he added, *he was giving them nothing to eat!*

Teddy returned to say that a small mail boat was coming down the river with a barge and could take us as far as Juba, where the Imperial Airways had workshops and could help with our repair.

The captain kept us thoroughly amused with stories of the river. On his last trip he had been towing a barge loaded with gunpowder, and his mate, a very slow-speaking Scandinavian, came to him during the night and in broken halting English said, "Sir - you - know - the - powder - boat - we - are - towing - behind - and - you - also - know - that - here - the - natives - walk - about - at - night - with - flaring - torches; - well - I think - one - of - those - natives - with - a - flaring - torch - is - walking - about - on - the - powder..." Before he got any further, the captain had rushed up on deck, jumped onto the barge, and with a well-directed kick sent the native and his torch into the river.

Lower down we picked up a cheery lad who was something to do with the Government educational control, and he invited us to stop with him at his place near the Congo border while we waited for our car parts to arrive. Here we had a wonderful rest and holiday for a week, during which I laid out a golf course, and, being the first to go round, held the record for a course for once in my life.

Everyone was being pressed into a campaign against the locusts, and I, noticing that if one was killed, the others became cannibals, had the brilliant idea of boiling some in arsenic, which I presumed when eaten would go on killing ad infinitum. Having spread these round the place I waited for results, but when I was told next day that two of the turkeys had died, did not offer my suggestion to the authorities.

Thanks to a most wonderful piece of service, and to the help of Imperial Airways, our spares arrived in seven days from the time we had sent our wire, probably quicker than we could have got them in a small town in England, and we were off again.

# Chapter 7 ~ Uganda ~ Kenya

Over the Nile for the last time, and we were in Uganda. The roads were good, we had no fear of rains, and we had had a good rest, but this did not make me any more popular with the other two, especially when I told them that funds were nearly at an end.

We were now travelling in easy stages, camping early, and after meals (which I cooked) I usually wandered off on my own, and one night was rewarded by seeing the wildest native dance I have ever seen. Crawling up a bank which overhung their dancing place, I saw their sweating bodies shining in the light of the huge fires they had lit. They charged at each other with their spears, and now and again one of them would fall. Whether they had actually been speared or were merely falling from exhaustion, I could not make out in the flickering half-light of the flames, nor did I stop very long, as I did not relish the idea of being discovered in my hiding place.

The same night, throwing wood onto our camp fire, I picked up quite a large snake but was luckily not bitten. John killed it before it could get away, and we found it to be a most deadly one.

Daylight showed wonderful rolling plains stretching on either side of us, with outlines of huge mountains, probably the Mountains of the Moon, etching the horizon away to the west.

Kitgum, Lira and M'bale were passed through, then on we went to Tororo, where we enjoyed the luxury of staying in a hotel, although our financial condition did not warrant this extravagance.

At El Doret we were entertained by the Vacuum Oil Company representative. Quite a crowd, including the late Captain Black, of air fame, who, I understood, was flying for one of the petrol companies, joined us, and then we pushed on into the gorgeous scenery of the El Dama ravine.

Here we visited the local District Commissioner's house and a very charming little lady invited us to stay the night, apologising for the fact that her husband was away on the locust campaign. We had a very cheery evening sitting round a huge fire, as it was cold at this altitude.

The following morning, being first up, I was wandering round the beautiful garden with the dogs, when I met a chap who told me he had been walking nearly all night, doing one of the locust jobs. I said I thought that if he came in, he would probably be welcome to breakfast, to which he replied that he hoped so, as it was his house.

If you will look at a map, you will see that we were almost on the Equator, about halfway between Cairo and Capetown, and nearly in the centre of the Dark Continent. The road lay, a long narrow strip, across the country, but nowhere was there a sign of natives or wild animals. Instead, a large notice fastened to a tree announced that there would be "A hunt ball at the Crossroads Inn on Saturday next."

At Equator station the light railway runs for a short distance exactly on the equator, the road crossing the raised track at right angles. We got our front wheels over, but with our long chassis we touched in the centre, and there we were, balanced on the equator. Finally we had to get out of the car and push it over into the Southern Hemisphere.

*The Equator*

We were now in the wonderful scenery of the Great Rift Valley, the sides of which towered close to us. We passed some the smaller lakes, the shores of some of which appeared at first sight to be made of pink coral, but proved on closer inspection to be the feeding ground of thousands of flamingo.

A long steady climb took us up the escarpment and into the gay town of Nairobi, with its fine hotels and wide streets.

Luckily for us, for our funds were now almost nil, I seem to have friends everywhere, for hardly had we got into the main street than someone turned up whom I had known in Singapore, and he put us all up. Incidentally, I give full marks to Nairobi for crazy driving; everybody seems to be permanently in a desperate hurry.

*Delamere Avenue, Nairobi*

Next day we started for the coast, enough money being grudgingly supplied by Teddy, whose remittance had arrived, for us to take the short cut, via the Athi Plains.

This road had been built, or rather marked out, by the Royal East African Automobile Association. Working with very little money under the guiding hand of their energetic secretary, Mr. Galton Fenzi, they had blasted a way through rocky outcrops by the simple method of making a huge fire on the rocks and when they were red hot, throwing water on them to make them split. Later, this route, as it competed with the railway line, had been allowed to go back to its primitive state, and those cars which had lately used it had each made a new track, so that the "road" was in some places over a mile wide.

Game was plentiful, and at one point we saw the astounding sight of a herd of buffalo, giraffe, zebra, and thousands of gazelle and ostriches running away from the advance of an oncoming train, while in the distance could be seen one of the Wilson Airways planes, our car taking up the foreground.

Relations between the party were now at breaking point, especially as I had suggested that Teddy should come to the rescue with some more of that remittance, and it seemed very obvious that the final break would come at Mombasa.

I was determined the expedition should go through to the Cape and offered to drop out and continue on a motor cycle if they would take the car through. John was willing, but Teddy was not, and it seemed inevitable that they would return together by boat.

To add to my troubles, I developed the worst attack of malaria I had yet had. In spite of this I foolishly insisted on driving, with the result that I knocked the tap off the oil sump on a rock. This damage was repaired by hammering a pencil into the hole.

Just before Tsavo we saw lion in the distance, which made off when we got really close. [The Ghost and the Darkness, 1996, was a movie based on the true story of two lions at Tsavo that killed 130 people over a nine month period, starring Michael Douglas and Val Kilmer.] The fever got worse, and I entered Mombasa lying in the back of the car, while they drove straight to the docks. I was able to sit up and join a conference as to what we should do next. Although our money was gone, I refused to sell the car or quit the trip, knowing I could do something when the fever left me.

Well, I told you I was always lucky; while I was still trying to convince them that things were not hopeless, a seaman strolled over to look at the car, and who should it be but the skipper of a tramp, whom I had known quite well when he had been on the China run.

He saw that I was pretty bad, and insisted on our going aboard for some whisky and quinine. That was the last I knew for two days, which I spent on my back on one of the bunks.

When I was fit to move, although still feeling terrible, I found that the other two had gone ashore and were staying with a junior member of the Vacuum Oil Company, and that an invitation had been left for me to join them.

The tramp steamer was due to leave, so, having thanked my friend, I staggered ashore and made my way to the house, where I again collapsed. I was getting better, though feeling frightfully weak and ill. My host was goodness itself, but informed me that he could not stick Teddy at any price, and as he still had most of his remittance and was expecting another, he was asked to leave. He had made friends with a man and his wife who wanted him to stay with them, and asked if he could take the car to carry his kit over there.

Three days went by, and I was feeling better but decidedly shaky. When I suggested that John should drive me over to the Vacuum Oil Company's office, I wanted to see if the company would frank us through the rest of the way, he told me the car had not yet come back...

I sent him off to fetch it, and he reported that Teddy refused to return it, and was holding it until we paid back what we had borrowed from him. Having received this discouraging information, he had been kicked out by Teddy's newfound friend, a huge fellow who, it was alleged, had been a well-known amateur boxer.

I went myself, with no better result. I got Teddy to come over and discuss the matter, but lost my temper badly when he refused to do anything but demand his money, and got still madder when he refused to fight, even after I had swung at his moustache.

Things were badly out of control, and much as it went against the grain, I eventually went to the police. Unfortunately I admitted that the car belonged to the expedition as a whole, and although I held the biggest share, they pointed out that it was probably as much his as it was ours and they could do nothing.

But, they said, possession being nine points of the law, if we could get hold of it, matters would be different, and they naively suggested that as soon as we could get it, they would assist us by enforcing the immigration law compelling us all to get out of Kenya in seven days.

This didn't seem much help, but that night we watched the house where Teddy was staying until we saw them all leave, then, breaking open the garage, we tried to start up the car, when we found that essential parts of the magneto and carburettor had been removed. The ground sloped away from the garage, and we managed to manhandle the car out and down to the side of a large canal or river bed, and I decided that I would chance running it over the bank on the slant and stopping it before it got to the water. This was done successfully, and the car was so well-hidden under the steep bank a little distance from the house that I knew it would not be found unless anyone specially looked there, and that was most unlikely, as the ground was hard and showed no tracks.

I had almost collapsed again, but next morning I got one of the local garages with a lorry to tow the car to their premises and left instructions for them to remake the necessary parts, but under no circumstances to fit them.

In the meantime the other party had gone to the police to report that their garage had been broken into and the car stolen, and I soon had the police asking what I knew about it. I told them that I had simply worked on their advice to get possession of the car, which did not seem to please them at all, and they issued an order under the immigration laws that we should either have to make a large deposit of money or leave the country in sixteen days. It would take ten of these to make the necessary parts.

When we came back from the police station, we found the others had made a raid on our quarters, turning our beds upside down, throwing all our clothes out of the window, and putting our hairbrushes into the bath.

By this time most of Mombasa knew some version of the facts, and the town was divided into two camps for or against us. The local magistrate seemed to be against us, though the political people were for us; however we received little but advice on which we could not act.

I believe it was the Town Clerk who sent for me, and when I turned up at the Courts, asked me what really was the trouble. I gave him my story, which didn't impress him much, despite the fact that he was a man with a lot of understanding, as his remarks showed. He asked me what it was I really disliked about our Number Three, and when I told him it was chiefly the moustache, and the moustache-trainer that he would put on in the morning even in the desert, he said he saw that reconciliation was impossible. He said he had once travelled in a cabin with a man who would suck the water off his toothbrush every morning, and he admitted he would gladly have killed him before the boat reached port, and it *was* the small things that counted.

The police remained neutral, disliking both parties, and constantly reminding us that we only had a few days to do something before we were deported.

John and I had written to our respective families asking for small loans, and when these arrived, we decided to leave Teddy and take the car straight from the garage over the border into Tanganyika [Tanzania]. As we went up the long main street to collect it, it dashed past us with Teddy driving. A car in front and another behind were full of his supporters, who howled at us and waved pickaxe handles.

That was the last I ever saw of the Rolls, and John's inevitable, "Well, now we *are* bitched!" seemed for once to be justified.

# Chapter 8 ~ Kenya ~ Tanzania

As I said, the last we saw of our car was as it disappeared down Mombasa High Street, and I got no further news of it until six years later, when I heard it was to be seen hard at work on the Kakemega Goldfields, nor have I ever met our Number Three again. If I did, I could laugh over that trip with him, for although I cannot forgive him for letting us down while I was on the sick list, I can realise now that I must have been pretty trying.

However, at that time I could very cheerfully have committed murder if I could have found him, but as he and his friends had disappeared and we only had three days left before the police descended on us, something had to be done. We officially reported the theft of the car to the police, who were not very sympathetic; no bar offered itself as a source of inspiration, and I found that John could not ride a motor cycle, so that idea was out.

With the small amount of cash that had come through from our people we decided to see if we could get some kind of vehicle to carry us on. Most of the samples had been left with us, and we thought we might be able to save something from the wreck.

Eventually we found and bought a T model Ford, which even at that date was prehistoric.

*[A Model T Ford]*

It had what the vendor called a safari body, that is a box-like affair, with boxes hanging over the wheels and acting as mudguards, and a flat-topped canvas roof, green with age, supported by two iron brackets behind and two in front, the whole thing looking rather like a rag-and-bone man's van.

In this we set out, and with only twelve hours to go before our zero hour, decided that if the police didn't see us, it would be better for all concerned. We kept hidden all day and started out just before dusk, keeping to the outskirts of the town. We rattled our way through the native quarters, disturbing the already roosting chickens, and came by a circuitous route to the new causeway. We knew that if we could get over this, we had a very sporting chance of not being stopped, as we could always run off the road into the bush if we heard a car approaching, and anyway the police really only wanted to see the last of us.

The causeway being clear, we made a dash over it, flat out at some 25 m.p.h. and found we could keep up a really fair average on the earth roads.

Later in the night we passed the station known as Mackinnon Road and decided to camp. Having run well off the road into the bush, we spent a most uncomfortable night, John curled up in the driving seat and myself draped over the baggage in the rear. Flaps of torn canvas, pulled down from the roof, shut out some of the noises of the night, but gave us very little sense of security against lions, which we understood were plentiful here. I felt particularly apprehensive as just before leaving England I had read "The Lions of Tsavo" and we were only a few miles from that spot, also I had seen the following in a local newspaper:-

## LIONS AT STATIONS

### Fight for Water - Uganda Railway Thrill

*Nairobi, Tuesday.*

*The latest thrill provided for passengers by the Uganda railway for Nairobi from Mombasa is the sight of prides of lions quarrelling around locomotive water tanks at wayside stations where the trains stop to replenish supplies after the long haul through the bush country.*

### Occupied Platform

*At Mackinnon Road station a few days ago four lions had possession of the platform when the train arrived. They were frightened off with difficulty, but returned immediately the train had gone, to lap water from the pools that had overflowed during watering operations. The Indian stationmasters at these lonely stations now beat petrol tins before venturing to leave their offices to deal with trains. Ticket collectors sometimes awaken passengers to see lions prowling in the thin bush behind the tanks.*

51

## Rhinos, Too

*On the Voi-Moshe branch line, where drought has been worst, rhinos are also frequent visitors, and station staffs have decided to remain behind locked doors at night.*

However, I must have slept, for I was awakened by a terrific grunting and growling. It was quite a few moments before I realised it was John, snoring happily with his six foot odd curled along the front seat and his feet sticking out under the canvas as a tempting morsel to any hungry lion that might be looking for breakfast.

Having got our cramped bodies to work again, we tumbled out and started to get a fire going, when I spotted a full-grown elephant watching us from not sixty yards away. This kind of thing happened, as you will learn, several times during my African safaris, and I give first prize to the elephant for camouflage, considering its bulk.

John saw it at practically the same time and made a leap for the front seat, while I dived through into the back of the car, only to meet him in a head-on collision in the middle. Scrambling round on the baggage, I applied my eye to a tear in the canvas, while John tried frantically to get the car started. It had other ideas, and in spite of my advice to choke it and then not to choke it, the engine remained obstinately dead.

Our visitor, however, did not approve of the noise we were now making and ambled lightfootedly away. As soon as he had disappeared I ran to the front and after vigorous swinging of the handle, in conjunction with the self-starter, the car burst into a riot of noise and vibration. Leaping in, we started off onto the road, passing several heaps of smoking dung, which proved that a fairly large herd of elephants had streamed past us during the night.

Our sole rations consisted of a loaf of bread, one tin of sardines, and a bottle of Marmite, and we made a satisfying meal off these before passing through Voi.

Here we stopped for a while, having a very welcome cup of coffee with the Indian stationmaster. He confirmed that lions were very plentiful in this district, and recalled the famous incident of the Indian stationmaster who rang up Nairobi to say that he was barricaded in the station office while two lions were walking up and down the platform, and would they send him immediately two bullets, as he had a rifle but no ammunition.

We crossed the Kenya border late in the afternoon and entered Tanganyika. At Moshi the Immigration officer told us he did not think he could allow us to enter the country without either a substantial cash deposit or some kind of guarantee. Anyway, it was too late to do anything that night, but we had better see him in the morning.

Crossing back into Kenya we started to make camp, but hearing a car coming, hastily ran over to the Tanganyika side and got behind some scrub, then hearing a car coming from that side, dashed back again into

Kenya, eventually making camp some distance off the track and well hidden.

In the morning we again ran into Moshi, and almost the first person we met was Heinz of the German party. He had left his confreres when they arrived at Juba and had come on alone. Although Tanganyika was under British mandate, he had had no trouble whatever in entering, and even offered to come to the Immigration office with us to see what he could do, as the officer in charge was a South African who spoke fluent German.

We all trailed down to the office, and after a lot of talk we were informed that nothing could be done until the Immigration Officer had wired Dar Es Salaam about us, one of the chief troubles being that I still had no passport.

However, we were allowed to stop in Moshi, and decided to camp with Heinz on the outskirts of the town. In the meantime I had wired to the Overseas League and asked if they would come to the rescue with some more finance.

We spent a lazy day admiring the wonderful scenery with occasional glimpses of the snow-covered saddleback crest of Mt. Kilimanjaro as the clouds blew away from its summit, and in the afternoon Heinz suggested that as the Masai natives here hunted both lion and buffalo armed only with spears, it was up to us as white men to show that we could do the same. Knowing nothing about it, I was quite game to try. Heinz, who was still posing as the tough colonial, ostentatiously put on knee boots, pointing out to me that he never wore socks, a fact which probably saved our lives, for long before we had walked to where the game could be found, he was limping so badly that we had to turn back, and he did the last part of the journey in bare feet, still proclaiming his toughness, until he stepped on a thorn, when he broke into voluble German, which may have been on the same subject, though I doubt it.

Next day we decided to take an inventory of our resources, the list reading:-

- One car, in very poor condition.
- Two tyres with tread.
- Three tyres without tread.
- Cooking gear. Nil.
- Arms and ammunition. Nil.
- One large hammer and two rusty spanners.
- Two sets of blankets.
- One rusty axe.
- Four sample bottles of whisky.
- Six sample bottles of cocktails.
- One sample case of surgical instruments
- One passport between the two of us, and very little money.

John thought that if he could only get into Northern Rhodesia, he could get a job in the mines there, but I was still for getting through to the Cape.

During the day we purchased a loaf of bread, sixteen eggs for a shilling, and a huge pineapple for fifty cents.

Having laid in supplies, it was necessary to start planning our programme, and this needed thought mixture, so we repaired to the Kilimanjaro Hotel bar. In these small towns the advent of a stranger is a matter of interest and we were soon the centre of an audience who listened to an edited account of our journey from London. It was here that we met Major Perkins, a staunch supporter of the Overseas League, and he promised to do all he could to assist us.

Later, John and I, feeling much more optimistic, strolled through the native village on our way back to camp, the market place looking particularly bright, as each native was compelled by law to carry a lamp, which, as they moved backwards and forwards, gave the impression of gigantic fireflies.

The subdued mutter of the village drums followed us back to camp and came with us into the land of dreams.

In the morning, nothing had come through from Dar Es Salaam, and one of our tyres was flat. It was while repairing this that we found the spokes of one wheel almost rotted through.

During the day we were made members of the local club, had some tennis, and enrolled quite a few members for the Overseas League.

Later, the Immigration officer sent a message to say we could proceed, and we decided to get away at daybreak, but afterwards he came up himself and told us that he had had a wire from Dar Es Salaam and we could not go yet after all.

Heinz was pushing on, so we camped once more, wondering what on earth was going to happen in the morning. When we got into the town there was no news, but Major Perkins promised to wire to the authorities on our behalf, and presently a message came through saying that money had arrived from the Overseas League but had been sent to Arusha, the next town on our route. We instructed the banks to get this sent to us at Moshi, and went back to camp again.

The morning looked very stormy, with huge clouds hiding Mt. Kilimanjaro. After a breakfast of eggs and a plunge in the river we went down town and having argued for hours, agreed to deposit forty pounds, Major Perkins very decently guaranteeing the rest.

We eventually got underway at three in the afternoon, first visiting the market and getting in supplies, with a big reserve of potatoes.

The first part of the run was through scrub country very well watered by rivers, which were fortunately bridged. We met the road superintendent en route, and he informed us that his car had been followed by two lions, and that he had travelled slowly to see how close they would come, and we should probably see them before we got into Arusha. However, there was no sign of them.

We spent a very pleasant evening as the guests of the padre at Arusha, and got on the road soon after dawn with a large supply of strawberries he had given us from his garden.

The road had just been remade, and signboards every half-mile advised all and sundry, "Mind your springs!" "Save your life!" "Make your own track!" etc. Another puncture just outside the town made us return, and we had a very cheery session at the Arusha Hotel, during which we somehow acquired a dog. The hotel claims to be exactly half way between Cairo and Capetown and the exact centre of Uganda, Kenya and Tanganyika.

*The Arusha Hotel*

Later in the evening, with the tyre patched up, we got going and camped close to Lake Manyara, witnessing a really glorious African sunset. African memories usually start with the recollection of the lengthening of the shadows of the hills and the curious change from gold and brown to deep purple before darkness blots everything out.

We were now in what is perhaps the finest wild game country in the world, and before going to bed, twice saw leopard, probably attracted to the camp by the small terrier that we had added to the party at Arusha.

The next morning I hoped to spend at a friend's place near Babati but on arrival at the Fig Tree Hotel, a small hotel built, so I understand, by Lord Lovelace as a centre from which to hunt, we found several people in the little bar and learnt to our horror that my friend had been killed by an elephant.

A rogue elephant had been damaging some of the native huts and the natives had come running to him asking him to shoot it. He was an experienced elephant shot, and had another well-known hunter staying with him, which makes it all the more incredible that he should have grabbed up his light gun instead of the elephant gun, and on top of that his friend yelled after him, "Have you got the right gun?" and heard him call back, "Yes." Dashing down to the compound he came right on the elephant, which attacked immediately and killed him, his light gun failing to stop it, and his friend only came on the scene in time to avenge his death.

While we were listening to this story, we heard a curious high-pitched scream - I cannot describe it as anything else - from our dog, which had been left in the back of the car just outside the window. I rushed out and was just in time to see a leopard dashing up a tree that almost overhung the hotel, with the dog in its mouth. At the first fork it turned to snarl down at me. By that time our friends in the bar came running out with their guns, and they dropped the leopard first shot, but our new partner was dead.

Our next day's run took us through magnificent scenery, the road running on a ridge that gave us glorious views of the country below us. Silent in the blazing sun lay vast plains on which nothing moved but the shadows of the clouds and the long necks of herds of giraffe as they fed on the umbrella-shaped trees with their amazing armament of spikes. The car boiled continually, owing to the thousands of locusts stuck in the front of the radiator, and we had to stop at nearly every river to add water, John using his shoe as a bailer.

After Kondoa Irangi we again made camp among the terrible thorn bush with its three-inch long spears, and had the greatest difficulty in getting any of the beastly stuff to burn. Using one of the four-gallon petrol tins as a sort of brazier we were eventually able to fry some meat that had been given to us at the last stop.

Dust followed us, blew up over us from the front wheels, and came in gusts over the sides as we shook and rattled along through the monotonous scrub-covered plains. At Dodoma we went to the railway station and filled our odd collection of tins and cans with water, then over to the hotel for some beer, where a notice offered two tame cheetah for sale, guaranteeing them to be docile and good pets, and finally went back on our tracks a little way for camp.

Camp was always a difficult proposition, for it had to be on a hill so that we could push the car off and get it started in the morning; it had to be near wood for the fire, and it also had to be near water, the combination of all three being very hard to find.

We usually stopped an hour or so in the small prosperous towns through which we passed and enrolled members for the Overseas League, as we got an excellent commission on these and at the same time felt we were doing a good turn, and I thought we should be able to finance ourselves through on this, the other agencies that we carried requiring time before commission could be expected.

We had now got together a collection of four-gallon petrol tins and I decided to stop for a day and convert these into frying pans, pots, and the other utensils that we required badly, so we made camp in a large valley by the Ruaha River. Game was plentiful, but we had no guns, and we saw so many succulent chops and steaks and game birds, who seldom moved far away at our approach, as though they knew they were safe from us.

We put in a hard morning's work, John sitting on a log with a typewriter balanced on petrol cans taking down letters which I dictated while I washed our small supply of clothing, then hung it round the camp and on the car, which made it look more than ever like a rag-and-bone man's collection van.

At Iringa we expected to get our immigration deposit back, but the officer in charge told us bluntly that we couldn't have it. John got his, "Now we are bitched" complex, and only brightened a little when I suggested that a visit to the bar might help. On the way down we were hailed from a garage, and were soon recounting the tale of our adventures. Our audience gradually grew, and it was suggested that we should move the party to where it could be lubricated. On the way, we were taken to see the remains of an old Rolls Royce which we thought might possibly be ours, as it was the only one that was reported to be in Tanganyika, but it wasn't ours.

We were introduced to the proprietor of the hotel, who proved to be the famous Zambesi White. I never quite discovered what he was famous for. His version was that he was the great white hunter of the Zambesi River, and that the natives there, in admiration of his prowess, had given him that name, but I afterwards learnt that the natives of the territory have the custom of knocking out most of their front teeth when they became hunters, and our host, having prosaically fallen down some stairs, had knocked out the same ritual front teeth, and this was really why the natives had given him this name.

Anyway, he had some excellent stories. One that particularly amused me was the tale of the elephant that walked into the town of Broken Hill. In those days, our host explained, every man was a hunter and kept his rifle loaded and ready to hand, so that when the elephant appeared in the main street it was met by a fusillade of lead and rapidly succumbed, not so much because it had been hit in any vital spot as because it was so full of lead that it sank under the weight. The local photographer, an opportunist of the first water, got to work, and one after another the citizens were photographed in heroic attitudes beside the carcass, including the barber, who, being about the only man in the place who did not possess a rifle, had to borrow one for the occasion. Later the barber came to England, and on the strength of the photograph he was acclaimed by one of the London papers as a big game hunter. His fame grew, and he told the story of his mythical hunt so often that he at last came to believe it himself, so that on his return to Rhodesia, he fell easily into the trap the local wags had laid for him. The game warden, the police, and a few friends met him on his arrival, and congratulated him on his hunting exploit, which, for the benefit of the Press, was supposed to have occurred some way out in the bush. He could not resist the temptation of further hero-worship, and once more repeated the tale, altering a few details to explain why they hadn't heard of it when he was living in Broken Hill. Then one of the audience stated flatly that he didn't believe it, and the barber, unaccustomed to having his story doubted, swore by all the gods that it was true. By adroit questioning, they made him confirm the story in detail and then reminded him there was no record of his having a licence at the date of his supposed elephant hunt, and therefore he owed the licensing authorities fifty pounds for a game licence and twenty-five pounds for a special elephant licence, or he would be considered an ivory poacher and would have to pay a heavy fine for shooting an elephant without a licence.

The evening stretched on in an endless row of tankards, the party getting merrier and merrier, with the exception of John, who was rapidly reaching the morbid stage. Zambesi White pressed us to stop at the hotel as his guests, and for the first time in several weeks we had a proper bath and bed. As usual after a visit to the font of inspiration, I was full of optimistic schemes, but poor John, who only wanted to stop his mattress revolving and brood on our bad luck, leapt up and before I could get to the point where we lived happily ever after, had me down on the bed with both his huge hands biting into my throat. A lucky heave landed us on the floor and soon a good stand-up fight was in progress, our host's best Birmingham ware [crockery] being kicked about among the overturned chairs and bedclothes. A hefty blow on John's befuddled brow ended the scrap, and we retired among the debris. Morning revealed a scene of wreckage, John with a badly cut eyebrow and two eyes that showed a wealth of colour round black centres, and myself with the knuckle of my right little finger smashed. Strangely enough the battle seemed to have cleared the air; we shook hands, I with my left, which John could hardly see, and then walked over to the local chemist to get patched up.

Having thanked our host and told him what a wonderful time we had had, we set off, as we had previously found that we should have to go to M'beya before our deposit would be returned.

# Chapter 9 ~ Tanzania ~ Zambia

Leaving the hotel, we followed the one main dusty street through the native market, where the stalls were mostly kept by Indians, who did not disdain to deal in quantities as small as one cigarette. We left the town and, descending the escarpment at a terrific speed owing to the complete failure of our brakes, we were once more in the African bush and would probably not meet another white man for some time. We crossed the long valley and started to climb, but not for long, as although the engine still made a satisfactory row, and we rattled as much as ever, we made no further progress until we had taken off the covering of the gear box and tightened up the bands with a rather bent metal cloakroom ticket that John had purloined from a London club in the dim distant past, and for some unknown reason carried with him as a sort of fetish like a lucky threepenny bit. Frequent use of this implement and a nail-file took us twenty-four miles further and up to twelve thousand feet, from which height we had a glorious view over country which, broken only by the narrow strip of road we had followed, was the haunt of thousands of wild animals, and much of which may not have been trodden by the feet of white man.

Having soaked in the atmosphere of the wide open spaces, we turned and went into the sausage factory that stood on the other side of the road. We enrolled the proprietor as a League member, were presented with a gift of tinned sausages and bacon, and moved on again, stopping briefly at Colonel Fawen's ten-thousand acre fruit farm, where, although the farm was nearly on the equator, he was trying out apples, not such an impossible idea as it sounds, as the farm was six thousand three hundred feet up.

From here a long gentle slope gave us respite from the racket of our engine, as we coasted down it for all the world like small boys in a soap box on wheels, even getting out to give the car a push over the next rise, the only spectators being a few monkeys.

We were admiring some of the wonderful scarlet blossoms of the flame-of-the-forest trees when one of our tyres went off with a terrific bang. Investigation revealed that the inner tube had blown right through the cover, and our primitive tools refused to budge the rim, which had rusted on. So, having wrestled with it for some time, we sat down to cool off, watching the brilliantly coloured birds that flashed across our view. Finally, Lady Luck produced a breakdown lorry that was going through to the mines, the driver of which, welcoming the chance of a rest, sat and watched us while [we] used his tools to remove the rim.

Still frequently adjusting the gears with our metal cloakroom check, we began climbing steadily again. Another blowout occurred on a steep rise, and John had to leap out and get a stone to put under the wheel to stop us rolling backwards before it could be repaired. The repair was achieved only after I persuaded John to part with a piece of his trouser-leg for patching, telling him that anyway shorts were the correct kit for the country, and we shuddered into the little mining town of M'beya.

It was a Saturday and apparently early-closing day, for the Immigration officer refused to return our deposit until Monday. Luckily the town boasted a source of inspiration, or should I say it was the only source of inspiration, for the town consisted almost entirely of one hotel, and we made our way there.

As we approached, our ears were assailed by a deafening noise. It sounded as though a free fight, a debating society, and a morris-dancing troupe were all hard at work. John got into conversation outside while I went through into the low-ceilinged barroom.

I arrived at the bar and a bearded apparition with bloodshot eyes rose from behind it and bellowed at me; "I'm Jem! I found the ruddy nugget! D'you know what I'm here for?"

I suggested that it might be to serve drinks, but he said "No! I'm here as chucker-out!" and with that he leapt over the bar and embraced me in a bear-like hug. Clutched together like a couple of dancers, we cannoned from table to table and ended up on the ground outside. Arriving there, we sat up, and my new acquaintance said;

"Well, that's that. We'd better have a drink."

So we elbowed our way back gain through the crowd that had gathered to see the fun, whereupon he went behind the bar and immediately repeated the entire performance.

John was sitting at a table with a long beer already in front of him and called to me to come over and join him, but Jem was now insistent that I should drink with him.

This time we got a drink, but before I was halfway through it, one of the miners came up to me and demanded, "You're a bloody Englishman, aren't you?" I admitted that I was certainly an Englishman, and it transpired that he had always wanted to fight a bloody Englishman.

The crowd seemed to think this an excellent idea, and before I knew where I was, a circle had been formed outside and I was in the ring with my opponent, who shambled round and round in the dust like a dancing bear. Jem was to referee, and had brought the bar clock out to time the rounds.

Fortunately for me, my adversary could see two of me and kept hitting the wrong one, and when I tapped him on the nose it bled copiously, whereupon he declared he had fought a bloody Englishman and the drinks were on him.

John, who had been on the outskirts of the ring, now came over, and I suggested that he should take my sparring partner in for a drink. He started to do so, but hardly had they entered the hotel together, the miner still wiping blood from his nose, when one of the other miners' wives rushed up, shrieking, "You drunken Englishmen come here and insult my guests!" and hit poor John a terrific bang on the ear and chased him round the bar.

Peace being eventually restored, I discovered that a fair-sized nugget had been found on the Lupa goldfields, and the alluvial workers, who all mined their own patch of ground, considered this a cause for celebration. The word had gone round, and they had all repaired to the hotel, generally known as the "snakehouse", and were hitting it up. The nugget, which was on view in the bar, acted for a while as a football, and a strenuous game was played round the tables until the owner raised the objection that a piece had been pinched off it, which was, however, found and restored. I heard later that when the nugget was sent out (presumably to a bank in a larger town, there being none here) it disappeared en route.

Jem and I were fast friends, and sat round the huge open fire yarning until the early hours of the morning.

The hotel proper is merely a bar and a dining room, and the visitors staying there sleep in small round huts, called *rondhavels*, at a little distance from the main structure. In the morning, we went on a round of these to assist at the rites of having a hair of the dog that bit us, and were invited to go gold-mining, shooting, fishing or merely to come and stay with almost everyone there.

We decided that a break would be a good thing, and accepted an invitation from a fellow known to all as Rip, who informed us that the track to his place on Lake Rukwa was so rough that a baboon had to use a walking-stick, but when you got there fish were five a penny and you could buy three women for a fish.

It was arranged that we should take a number of the miners on board our car, and Rip's, and drop them off opposite their workings in the hills as we descended the valley. Everyone had to take a few bottles along so that they could ease off the booze before getting down to work again, with the result that at each point a halt was made until the bottles had been drained.

We were now off the main track in wild, boulder-strewn country. Bush fires burning on the crests of the hills at night looked like fiery comets, while lions roared quite close at hand.

Rip was driving ahead of us, and we did our best to keep up, but the only time we saw him was when he stopped for a drink at one of the huge brick churches that had been built by the White Fathers as the mission headquarters. These wonderful buildings are designed by the Fathers themselves, and their converts, after first making the bricks, build these often immense structures, which appear wholly out of place in the surrounding bush.

Two more bad blowouts in the rear tyres held us back, so that it was already dark when we came to a dry river bed. The car went down the bank alright, but refused to climb out the other side. Successive attempts backing up the near bank and rushing at the other side failed to get us out, and we had to unload the car. I then backed the car as far as possible up the river bank we had just come down and made a dash across the river bed itself, where John was ready to push behind. We were nearly out when he yelled, "Lion!" and made a dash for the trees. Looking behind, I could see a fully grown lion regarding us from a little way up the river bed. By this time the car had lost its forward momentum and, the brakes failing to hold, I was going slowly backwards down the bank towards the lion.

Now, I don't know if you know the old T model Ford, so I must explain that the first and reverse gears are operated by simply pressing pedals, so that one can change from one to the other merely by pressing alternate feet on the respective pedals, and this is what I did.

*[The pedals of a Model T Ford - Clutch, Reverse, Brake]*

After about a mile, I cooled down, connected up our hooter [horn], normally voiceless, with odd bits of wire, switched on the lights, and making as much noise as possible, drove back, to find John still perched aloft but no sign of the lion.

We arrived at camp well after dark, and found Rip and his pals, Danny and Bill, getting down to clearing the last of the bottles we had brought with us. Bill seemed to have wandered all over the world in his search for gold, and kept us amused with stories of his experiences, while Danny, who had been left out of the "snakehouse" party, returned to M'beya on his own to repair the omission, stopping here and there on the way, as we afterwards learnt, to collect and take back with him a large number of people we had brought out. Bill told us that in his opinion, the whole of the shores of the lake on which we were camped were gold-bearing.

We slept that night in the rustling grass huts that had been built for us, and in the morning went down to the river which drained into Lake Rukwa to watch the natives employed by Rip netting fish. The fish, when caught, were dried on crude racks in the sun and then sent out to the mines for the boys working there. Up to four hundred fish were caught in a day, and the stench of their drying defies description.

That evening we went down to the lake shore, and having borrowed one of Rip's guns, I dropped an antelope with my first shot. The lake itself was simply seething with crocodiles and we shot six of these beastly animals at the waters edge without making the slightest impression on the rest. Further out in the centre of the lake, a school of hippo were grunting and making loud flatulent sounds after the manner of their kind.

The brief African dusk was gathering and it was now drinking time for the game, who seemed to recognise some kind of licensing hours. First came the gazelle, Thomson's and Grant's, their white tails continually on the move. Further away we could see the darker hue of bush-buck, then a herd of trotting zebra, and as we climbed out of the lake basin, we could see thousands of different species of antelope grazing towards the water, while overhead huge flights of flamingo flew in wedge formation, the steady beat of their enormous wings going whoosh! whoosh! as they passed over us. Waterfowl, also in formation, flew high above them, looking like fast fighting planes protecting the bombers represented by the flamingo and larger fowl.

Rip had to have meat to feed his boys, and without moving from our vantage point he brought off four fine long-range shots, dropping his game dead each time, and then took a snap shot at a running reedbuck, which carried on for some distance to disappear with a terrific leap in some small scrub. Rip asked us to collect it while he got the truck, which we had left a little way back. We couldn't find it, and when he returned we told him he must have missed it, at which he was most indignant, and said he had shot it in the throat, just under the jaw. Finally he walked straight up to where it was lying, its protective colouring having completely hidden it from our unpractised eyes, and sure enough, the bullet had entered exactly where he had told us.

On the way back we found a pelican in difficulties; it had, I think, torn its wing on one of the sharp spikes of a thorn tree, and Rip caught it and brought it back to camp. By the time we arrived there, the others were already punishing the bottle, and insisted on giving our new pet a generous drink, whereupon it chased us all out of the long hut where we had our meals, its huge beak with the horny pointed tip snapping together with a resounding bang close behind the seats of our pants as we dived through the doors and the openings left for windows.

Lion, hippo, hyena, jackal and other wild game set up an evening chorus round the camp as soon as the sun set, and I did not envy the White Father who visited us one night on a pushbike and then rode off cheerfully along the rough native track to visit a native who had been badly mauled by a leopard, but he seemed to consider it all part of his job, which included a great deal of doctoring.

We spent most of our mornings patching up our transport, lazed through the heat of the afternoon, watching the brilliant little blue birds flitting about the camp, and went shooting in the evening. Occasionally we tried, without success, to catch some of the fine fighting tiger-fish that lived in the lake. Our failure was perhaps due to the fact that we were worrying far more about crocodiles than fishing.

It was a pleasant interlude, but at last we decided it was time to be in on our way back to M'beya, so we said good-bye and made the return journey without further adventure.

At M'beya our deposit was returned to us, all in shillings, and with two large bags of these parked under the seat we felt unnaturally rich, as we pushed on through monotonous country to Chinsale and Lubwa Mission.

My broken knuckle had been giving a good deal of trouble, and it was practically impossible for me to swing the car in the mornings, so Doctor Brown of the mission station offered to fix it up for me. He insisted I should go under chloroform, and several of the sisters turned up to administer it and watch the operation. John always accuses me of having given a very obscene account, while under the anesthetic, of a mythical affair with a German lady, and I have never to this day been able to discover whether I actually did so or not. Certainly my nurses treated me with the greatest of courtesy while I was recovering, and gave no indication that their modest ears had been outraged, but John will have it that their kindness was due to admiration of my account.

I was feeling pretty bad after the operation, and gladly accepted the invitation of the District Commissioner to stop over with him for the night. He told us some interesting stories of his district, including the grisly tale of the local chief belonging to the House of the Crocodile, who, like many others, wished to show off greatness on the approach of authority, and had his meeting-house thatched with women's breasts, then, finding this gesture of goodwill was not appreciated, called in his vassal chiefs and had them executed as scapegoats.

He also told us that one night while he was on his rounds he was camping in a light open tent and a lion had pulled a blanket from the bed on which he was lying and had walked off with it.

Next day we decided to push on in spite of the fact that my hand was still troublesome and I had to call in at the mission on the way to have it put in splints.

Coming presently to a very sharp slope where we knew neither the brakes nor the gears would hold us, we hit on the ingenious plan of tying a large tree-trunk to the back of the car, thinking that it would drag on the ground and so retard our progress, but as soon as we started moving, it came bounding after us at such a rate that it was only by going flat out that we managed to keep ahead of it. When we got to the bottom it jammed and brought us up with a sharp jerk, whereupon our front spring snapped. We repaired this with a baulk of wood lashed under the chassis, and thereafter got the full benefit of each bump, which, added to the heat and dryness, loosened all the spokes in our wheels, so that each one, as it took the weight of the car, gave out its own particular squeak, like a Chinese burial cart.

One evening, camped in a small clearing amid tall elephant grass, I was happily cooking an antelope steak that had been presented to us, idly talking to John, who sat on the back of the car smoking his pipe and watching the shadows lengthening over the plain, when there was a rustle in the dry brittle grass, a deep coughing grunt, and a tawny shape leapt straight across the clearing.

The mind works curiously on such occasions, for although I had had time in the brief glimpse I caught of it to see that it was a lion, and made rapidly for the only possible shelter, the car, I still balanced the frying pan and steak with infinite care and am sure I didn't even spill any of the gravy. Although we couldn't see where the animal had gone, and had been told that only a man-eater would approach a camp, we enjoyed a hearty meal and slept without a thought of danger.

The following morning, when we got to the road - for we had gone a little distance off it to camp - we were in time to meet a sad procession carrying the dead and mauled body of a white man. He had been killed by a lion not half a mile away from our camp, and I shall always be convinced it was the lion who had leapt so boldly across our fire...

Our next stop was at a very interesting farm where trees were being grown for their essential oil. The owner, a friend of John's, told us that he had no love for long-distance tourists. Some time before, a motor cycle expedition had stopped with him for several days, and he had made them welcome and, when he had to visit a part of the estate some distance away, had told them to make themselves comfortable and do as they liked. Hardly had he started off, when his native boy came running after him to say that his guests were packing up all the small articles of value about the place into their sidecar and were preparing to make off with them.

Before we left in the morning we picked up an official of the Public Works Department and the Royal Mail Van. We were having considerable difficulty with our transport, but between them they kept us going for some time. They eventually became disgusted with our car, and offered to take us on as passengers, but we elected to stay with the old Ford.

It was surprising to look back to the days when we had a super car and equipment, and to remember how we used to curse and argue, whereas now we merely vied with each other in singing ribald extemporaneous verse dealing with each of our misfortunes, or roared with laughter when another bit fell off the car. I have often noticed that when one really is up against it, one has no time to moan, and can see some funny angle in the most frightful mishap.

And so we gradually worked southward, occasionally meeting people but more often having only the wild game for company, getting a terrific kick out of such sights as the two magnificent roan antelope which stood right in our path one day and hardly bothered to move as we passed them, or a wild pig scuttling off into the bush, which left us discussing how we should enjoy some pork chops if we had a gun and could hit it, and if we had some pots and could cook it.

We were again in thorny bush country, and my log shows a record of twenty-two punctures in twenty-one miles. I admit that this took some laughing off, but while we were mending the twenty-second of these, one of the celebrities of the Cape-to-Cairo trail turned up and informed us that we were close to his place, and took us back for my first introduction to *dop*, or Cape brandy.

We learnt afterwards that his fame spread far and wide, and he was always known by his native name of Chirupuru, which when interpreted meant "Whip them". He had settled here in the early days and had built himself a fine rambling homestead, and it was rumoured that the long barn-like structure behind his living quarters housed the finest harem to be found in Africa.

Before sampling the *dop*, I repaired our last puncture, but hardly had I taken my first sip when a loud bang heralded the departure of one tyre from all spheres of usefulness. The native boy who had been pressed into service had pumped it too high, the sun had completed matters, and the tyre was now blown into fragments.

In the evening we walked round the splendid orange groves enjoying the subtle perfume of the trees that here bore both fruit and flower at the same time. I don't know if it was a peculiarity of these particular oranges, but if a finger nail was drawn across the golden skin the oil which spurted from the scratch was so inflammable that it could be ignited with a match.

Our host, mellowed by his own brandy, importuned me to bring to the notice of the House of Commons the evidence he had collected for the Young Commission, concerning the stealing of land from the natives, and this I solemnly promised to do on my return.

The rows of orange trees were marked at each end with a number strung in an old tyre - yes, you have guessed it; one was our size and was presented to us when we left.

67

Lions roared round our camp at night and punctures and breakdowns held us up during the day, but we came at last to Kapiri M'Poshi, where we saw the railway again. The last we had seen was one running to the coast fifteen hundred miles behind us.

We became extravagant and stopped at the really fine little hotel, which was one of the three buildings that made up the town. Wonder of wonders, in the backyard stood an old car, exactly the same model as ours, and, better still, the proprietor gave me permission to take a few parts off it, as it had been abandoned years before. When he saw the parts I had taken he remarked that it would have been easier to take parts off ours and put them on his.

As we had no clock, no watches, no calendar and no speedometer, time and distance had come to mean nothing to us, and we lightheartedly decided to go miles out of our way up to the copper belt to see a friend of John's. One camp en route remains in my memory; we were at last among trees that were more than three inches thick, but most of them were mere shells, white ants having hollowed them out leaving only the bark and a thin layer of wood. A wooden hut by which we made camp was also merely a shell, and we used the remains to make a bonfire that must have been a beacon for miles. We played with this for some time, and when we came to move our kit, which we had put on the ground, found that the white ants had already started work on it.

Passing B'wana M'kuba gold mine, which was then deserted, the undulating corrugations of the road made by the mine lorries proved too much for the iron stays that supported the front of our hood [roof]. They snapped off, the roof fell on us, and that was so rotten that our heads went through it. This only gave rise to more merriment and we drove for [a] while with our heads sticking through the hole.

Ndola proved to be the biggest town we had seen since Mombasa, and John's friend entertained us royally, even taking us to the pictures in the evening. Next day we appointed several agencies and enrolled a number of League members.

One of the curiosities of the town and the surrounding country were the huge ant heaps some thirty feet in height. Our host had evicted the occupants of one of these, and had it hollowed out, and it made an excellent cool store room. The earth from these ant beds made an extraordinarily good surface for tennis courts, and was also used for greens on the golf course.

Our car was patched up at the mine, and we back-tracked once more to Kapiri M'Poshi and got onto the all-red route again, so called because, with the exception of Egypt, it passes exclusively through British territory. [Maps with territories marked in red belonged to the former British Empire.]

At Broken Hill, named after Broken Hill in Australia and not from any local topographical feature, we had a wonderful evening as the guests of the C. I. D. and the North Rhodesian police, who kept us up till the early hours listening to our adventures.

Before we got to Lusaka, which was later to become the Northern Rhodesian [Zambian] capital, one wheel collapsed and new spokes had to be hacked from a tree. The pinning presented a difficulty which was solved by burning holes with an iron rod in the ends of the spokes, and then pinning the outer rim onto them with live 303 cartridges, which for no reason that I can remember, we had with us. This strange repair took us into town, though I expected at any moment to hear the rear wheel behaving like a Catherine wheel. A car wrecking yard was kindly put at our disposal and a howling dust-laden wind nearly froze us to death as we worked making three old wheels we had found into one sound one, an unenviable job, for as soon as we got all but the last spoke into position, the whole lot would collapse and would have to be laboriously started again. The pinning holes in the rim had to be enlarged, the motive [electrical] power to work the drill being provided in a supremely Heath Robinson manner by a very large native mounted on the frame of a pushbike who pedalled for all he was worth to drive the belt between his rear wheel and the drill.

It would tax a more talented pen than mine to convey any idea of the country through which we were passing, not to describe its wonders, but to convey the endless monotony of colour and repetition of hills and scrub that only at night-fall became glamorous as the brown and gold turned to rich purple and dusk somehow brought with it a sense of Africa's vastness.

The only relief from the brown dusty earth and parched-looking trees was when we came to a river, such as the Kafue, where huge islands of reeds floated down with the current, looking unbelievably green by contrast. A many-spanned bridge carries the railway across and the hotel runs a ferry alongside it, consisting of a platform floated on empty petrol drums.

On this we perched the car, only to learn that there would be a charge of five shillings, so off it came again, and we made a long detour to cross by the Government ferry, only to be told, when we got on board, that they also charged five shillings.

That night we camped on the high banks of the river and before turning in, did some stocktaking; the resulting list was:-

- Two tyre levers.
- One repair outfit.
- Two broken spanners.
- One cloakroom check.
- Two jacks.
- One pump.
- Half a petrol tin as fireplace.
- Half a petrol tin as pot.

- Half a petrol tin as frying pan.
- A quarter of a petrol tin as griller.
- The tops of several tins as plates and toasters.

The backboard of the car acted as a table, and then we had our samples (excluding the whisky), our sole camp illumination being supplied by the tiny electric lamp on a long arm used for looking down patients' throats, which belonged to our sample case of surgical instruments.

The front seat lifted out, and by swivelling the back of the seat into a horizontal position from where it was attached to the sides, we were able to make our beds and lie full length on the floor.

As I mentioned before, we always stopped on hills so as to be able to push the car off and get it going in the morning. This particular night we had camped on the river bank, which sloped suitably, and John had curled himself up on the driving side with the top gear left in, to make more room. During the night he jammed his foot on the self-starter, which rolled us off the top of the bank and sent us careering down towards the river. The back of the seat was over us, preventing us from jumping out, and by sitting up we could only just reach the steering wheel. John managed to hang onto this and turn us at right angles to the water, while I climbed out of the back, ran alongside and took charge. We spent the rest of the night at an uncomfortable angle on the bank, and in the morning found one tyre flat. Having repaired this, much swinging of the starting handle and boiling water in the radiator got the engine going, but by then another tyre was down, and by the time that was repaired the engine had stopped, and we had to press some buxom native women into service to push us off.

Camp after camp was made and broken, most of them enjoyable and some exciting. Game often came quite close to us, and we gradually accepted the fact that throwing clods of earth at them was a sound means of defence.

Those evenings round a brisk fire after a satisfying meal and with a pipe going, chatting about the difficulties of the day and speculating on whether we should enter Capetown, rolling a wheel each, as sole remnants of the car, are among my pleasantest memories.

Alarms, such as when the wires of our horn suddenly fused, filling the hot night with raucous noise and nearly setting fire to the car, and we, being nocturnal nudists by force of circumstances, were almost eaten alive by mosquitoes in trying to stop the row and put out the fire, were frequent, but only provided a topic of more merriment.

We were following the railway line, but the country was still completely wild and we met few white men, while most of the natives were employed on road and railway construction. Crude signs indicated that farms lay close by, and I wondered idly what stories were behind such curious place-names as "Far enough", "No Further", "Here I Stop" and "The Last Day".

Before arriving at Livingstone, we had six more punctures, and after the last we stopped outside for general clean-up before entering the town. We visited the Post Office, where we found letters which conveyed to us that as far as any of our sponsors were concerned we could consider that we did not exist.

Our car caused a great deal of interest, the spectators including a policeman from Southern Rhodesia who told me in conversation that I hadn't a hope of getting any further without a passport. I had crossed five countries without one, but he was so emphatic that I thought I had better get one.

Actually this passport business is a most curious affair. I presume that originally they were issued to assist the traveller and the front page states in no uncertain terms that, "I (here follows a most impressive list of the designations of the governor or person issuing the passport) request and require in the name of His Britannic Majesty [George V] all those whom it may concern to allow the bearer to pass freely without let or hindrance, and to afford him every assistance and protection of which he may stand in need. Signed by the command of... etc. etc."

With a document like that from so notable a personage, you'd think that you could get anywhere without trouble, but what happens when you present it to the officials? They rudely paw it over, ask embarrassing questions, check up on the data which describes you, and stare coldly at you because you generally bear very little resemblance to the photograph inside. Having done all this and been grudgingly satisfied, they put a blurred stamp on the thing and very often add injury to insult by charging you for it.

In my case I didn't even ask to be "afforded every assistance and protection" but merely to "pass freely", and it seemed that this couldn't be done unless the Governor of Rhodesia asked nicely for me.

I went to the end of the town where a converted shop served as a police station and requested to be issued with a passport. I explained that I had come on a long trip and had lost my passport. It transpired that a wire had come through from Kenya concerning a Mr. Oldfield, who had left an expedition in Mombasa and sailed for India, and the police appeared to think that I was Oldfield, but I pointed out to them that I couldn't be, because if I were I should be in India, which they admitted seemed reasonable.

Told to go to a room at the back of the building and see the issuing officer, I knocked on the door and was bidden to enter. I did so, and a figure writing busily with its back towards me grunted "H'm?"

"I want a new passport. You see I've..."

"Get the hell out of here! I've told you you can't have one!"

"But hang it! This is the first time I've been here!"

He wheeled round and at once became profuse in his apologies. It seemed that someone or other was pestering him daily for a passport he could not issue, and when I arrived he had taken it for granted that it was his usual visitor. He proved to be an extraordinarily pleasant person, and in his anxiety to make amends for his rudeness, barely listened to my reasons for not having a passport, but told me to go at once and get two photographs and come back in the afternoon, when he would fix it up.

Livingstone didn't possess a passport photograph expert, but the local chemist came to the rescue by extracting a camera from his stock in the window and taking a whole roll of films of me draped against the splendid creeper-ornamented verandah at the back of his house. These were developed and two copies were printed of the one he thought best.

In the afternoon the friendly officer had gone on patrol, but had left instructions about me, and a charming young lady decided that I was five feet ten inches, had blue eyes and fair hair, and was born on the First of April, which I wasn't. Having entered these particulars on the passport, she then signed it for the Chief Secretary, and I could "pass" and "be afforded".

Next came the Customs, and this was a pleasant town for the chap in charge seemed to think we had done a wonderful trip, and having looked at our car and equipment, stated that not even the keenest Customs officer could put any value on it, so it was impossible to work out any duty. Better still, he gave us a letter to this effect, which carried us the rest of the way.

Formalities over and stores bought, we were off again on the first tarred road we had seen since leaving Cairo, and soon ran the few miles out to where the highest bridge in the world spans the Zambesi River just below the Victoria Falls.

# Chapter 10 ~ Zimbabwe ~ South Africa

We spent some time enjoying the wonder of the falls, a sight that in my opinion cannot be equalled anywhere in the world. Below us the mighty Zambesi, which at the top of the falls is over a mile wide, was restricted by the narrow walls of the canyon to probably not more than a hundred feet, or so it seemed to us from the height of the bridge. The water seemed to move slowly in vast swirls that somehow gave the impression of terrific power. The roar of the falls was terrific, and it is said that film of spray can be seen from a point over forty miles away.

*Victoria Falls*

Crossing the bridge into Southern Rhodesia, we turned off the road, following the light railway line that carries sightseers to the wonderful Victoria Falls Hotel, and picked a marvelous camping place above the falls and within a few yards of the Zambesi, just where the water began gathering speed for its leap down the Devil's Cataract. Behind us was the famous baobab tree on which every visitor seems to have cut his initials.

By the light of the full moon we walked through the rain forest, so called owing to the constant dripping of the trees which catch the spray sent up by the falling water. The forest clothes one side of the cleft which forms the Victoria Falls, the water tumbling over the other side then running out at right angles. To me this forest seemed the most tropical I had seen in Africa. Huge trees are laced together by gigantic creepers, tree-ferns and brilliant flowers grow profusely on any ledge they can find, mantling the tree trunks and the ground in colour. Everything dripped with the warm moisture caused by the clouds of spray, which in the moonlight looked like silver dust, and a moon rainbow continually spanned the falling water in its mad dash over the brink. Here again height made the water appear to fall slowly, looking like a white lace curtain on which the rocky islands on the far bank threw grotesque shadows.

For some time we walked, silent and enthralled, then threaded our way back, dodging under fallen giant trees, whose tops were still held from touching the ground by the mass of growth, and among the huge palms. The whole place formed the counterpart of my childhood dreams of an enchanted garden; the deep roar of the falls was obviously the roar of some giant trapped in the crevasse below, and to heighten the illusion, we disturbed a troupe of dog-faced baboons, who sat on their haunches or ran up tree trunks, following our every movement with their eyes, and looking like gnome servants of the monster below. Enormous baobab trees, their tendril-like branches clothed in what looked like very loose elephant skin, stood about in spooky attitudes, like personifications of that well-known villain of the advertisement hoardings, Oil-Brag, while from the silver Zambesi came the curious deep grunt of the hippo.

We crept back to our camp, feeling rather like the Babes in the Wood, and found that the small brown monkeys had paid us a visit, throwing things about and commandeering our supply of eggs, the dry and empty shells being strewn about the camp.

Two very enjoyable days were spent here before setting off to Wankie. We had been told of a short cut that would save us forty miles, but wished we had never taken it, as no attempt had been made to alter the natural gradients, so that our progress consisted of a series of rushes down steep hills, crashing into the loose stones at the bottom, and weary struggles up the other side.

We were cordially entertained at the Miners' Club, and learnt that Wankie was one of the largest coal mines in southern Africa. At that time, however, the pit heads were silent, and some mathematician worked out for us that owing to the terrific operating costs it would be cheaper to bring Welsh coal to the dump rather than get coal to the surface.

Things were going smoothly, the road had improved after Wankie, and I personally was in great spirits, in fact so great that I started knocking the hand-throttle of the car full open while John was driving, whereupon he promptly knocked it back again. I was under the impression that he was entering into the spirit of the thing, but suddenly he took a swing at me, knocked out part of the windscreen, opened the throttle to the full and let go of the wheel, so that we ended up deep in a thorn bush.

Having got the car out, we both felt definitely foolish, but neither would apologise. One of the tyres being flat, we started to make camp, both wandering off in different directions to collect the lumps of coal that lay on the surface, then building a fire and sulking in front of it, until suddenly I started laughing and we were friends again.

Steep dusty gradients took us through the Mica Hills, small specks of mica glistening like gold on the rough track, and then into Dett, where I told John we should end anyway, but he didn't see the pun and I didn't stress it. Here the car was subjected to the indignity of being put in a cage and thoroughly sprayed to destroy any tse-tse fly we might be carrying.

A bad blowout in the sandy bed of a dry river that we were following recalled our desert crossing, the resemblance being increased by the terrific heat. Here we found a lone individual resting in the shade of one of the river banks, and we picked him up and took him with us as far as Lupane, where we camped near a waterhole, one of a chain which was all that was left of a river. Others were also using this spot, and I made my first acquaintance with the Boer farmer. A large lorry contained Mother, Father, and three colossal sons, who came over to see us in the evening. Only one of the sons spoke English, the rest of the family speaking Afrikaans. They were on their way back from a journey to the copper belt, he told us, and having reached this spot could not get their lorry to start again. They had been here for three days, and seemed in their slow, heavy way to be prepared to stop there for ever.

John and I went over to see what we could do, and having inspected their engine found that their sump had been filled with heavy gear-oil. It was only necessary to drain this out and replace it with the proper oil to get them going again.

Bulawayo proved to be a fine flourishing town with imposingly wide streets. There is a legend that when Cecil Rhodes was planning the town he was asked what width the roads should be, and when he replied that they should be wide enough to turn in, this was taken to mean that they should be wide enough to turn a wagon with a full span of sixteen oxen.

We were the guests of the police, who seemed to be divided into two strongholds, those who were town police and those who patrolled the vast areas of Southern Rhodesia, and it appeared to be a point of honour that a patrolling officer, when in town, should endeavour to beat up one of his town brethren.

During the course of a hectic evening, I christened our car "Hoo B. Ray", which was solemnly painted on the bonnet, its interpretation being "Hoo-bloody-ray, we've got so far!"

Gwanda and Fort Nicholson were the next towns, and then Beit Bridge, across the Limpopo River, the gateway into South Africa, but before we got there another spring collapsed and had to be replaced by a wooden block.

The Customs and Immigration authorities passed us through without trouble, and opened the gate in the close-meshed wire fence to let us into the last country we had to go through on our way to Capetown.

Here we picked up a passenger for Messina. As he was a very large man I had to travel on the running board, and as the night was bitterly cold I arrived in the town with a really bad go of malaria. Our passenger assured me that the best cure for this was *dop*, and he, John and the proprietor of the hotel, whose guests we were, came to my room to see the cure work, which it did to such effect that I have never felt quite so ill in all my life, having such a bad head in the morning that there was no possibility of thinking about the fever.

The roads were now good, and we were making excellent time, the car climbing through the beautiful gorge at Louis Trichardt as though it knew it was getting near the end of its journey.

One humorous incident occurred before we got into Pretoria. We were travelling on a Sunday, and were meeting the Boer farmers on their way to church. Their mode of transport was often original, the best example being somewhat like a chariot. It had been made by taking the back of an old-fashioned car with seat and cushions complete and fixing this on a high axle to which car wheels and tyres were attached; this equipage was drawn by undisciplined wild-looking horses, driven at a sporting pace by a bewhiskered farmer dressed in a long black coat and soft hat. His wife sat on the far side of the seat and between them were several stodgy children.

We found that at our best pace we were just slightly faster on the level than they were, though they would gain on the up-grades. Earth tracks ran alongside the road proper, and they used these, sending up clouds of dust, while we stuck to the corrugated road. From our point of view the race was distinctly a joke. However they wouldn't enter into the spirit of the thing at all but kept up a fast trot, the driver's luxuriant growth of whiskers blowing back over his shoulder. Jolting ahead on a down-grade, we were waving back to them and making signs that we would give them a tow, when bang! went our crazy wheel, and they galloped past without even deigning to look at us.

We did not stop at the pretty town of Pretoria, its streets gay with the mauve flowers of jacaranda, but carried on straight through to

Johannesburg, camping some ten miles outside the town, beside the wonderful tarred road lined with shady trees.

I walked to one of the small stores near the camp and telephoned to a friend of mine, to let him know we were arriving the following morning, and he invited me to stay with him, John also getting an invitation from a doctor friend of his.

We appeared to be travelling at a terrific pace now that we were on a good surface, but smart-looking cars, mostly of American make, went flashing past us, although many of them slowed down to watch our strange vehicle. One driver stopped us and took us into the Halfway House Hotel to hear our story.

I remarked on the wildness of the country, considering that we were now close to the biggest town in South Africa, especially the huge stones that littered the countryside, and he said that God had made the country in six days and thrown stones at it on the seventh.

My friend in Johannesburg, Mr Castley, was the motor editor of the "Star".

*John Castley*

Some years before we had met in the Dutch East Indies when he and another man had been doing a world tour on B. S. A. motor cycles. While we were in Java together he had taken several photographs of me, and curiously enough had taken some to Africa with him. These he had used in the motor editorial the evening before, so that on our arrival we found we were quite famous, and there was a large crowd to welcome us outside the "Star" offices.

Jo'burg entertained us for several days, and during the time we were there, everyone seemed to go out of their way to lend us cars or show us the sights.

It is a wonderful city, quite unlike any other I have visited. The busy streets run in a kind of gridiron system, the traffic being controlled exclusively by robots [traffic lights]. South Africa being bi-lingual, the words "Go" and "Ry" have to be painted on the green lights, or else the Afrikaaner would ignore the signals on the plea that he did not understand English.

*The Market Square, Johannesburg*

But the most wonderful things here are the mine dumps, far more wonderful to look at, in my opinion, than the Pyramids. It is almost impossible to give an impression of their size, and I understand they are a source of considerable annoyance to the inhabitants, as the fine dust from them blows continually over the town. They have, however, one use; they make excellent landmarks for incoming aircraft, as I could see during a flight I was invited to make in an American W. A. C. O.

At last it was time to leave, another thousand miles would see the end of our trip, but before we got away, our old friends from the German expedition turned up. After leaving the Nile, they had driven down to Mombasa and there taken ship to Laurenco Marques and had then made their way through the Kruger National Park to Johannesburg. They were staying as the guests of the Castle Brewery, and we spent some very cheery times with them and their hosts.

The German community were making a great fuss of them, and a dinner was given in their honour at the German Club, which I attended. Being very fair-haired, I was congratulated many times by mistake, being taken for a German, but had usually got well into the proffered stein of beer before being found out.

One day was spent in Natal Spruit watching car racing. I got into the centre of the course in a very good position to see excellent racing by borrowing a cinematograph camera and turning the handle at anything that looked exciting. In this way I met anyone of interest, and had a wonderful time. It was unfortunate that I had no film.

Rains had been falling in Jo'burg, and we found the road out was in many places under water. Horst, Heinz, Beppo and Castley came out as far as the Flying Club to see us on our way, the Germans arranging to catch us up in the next three days so that we could enter Capetown together.

Noticing an old tyre that somebody had thrown away the other side of a fence, John crawled through to get it, further ruining his last pair of trousers. However, it was worth the sacrifice as it was better than any of ours, so into the back it went, ready for the next blowout.

We were making excellent time and soon passed through the towns of Parys, Vredefort, Kroonstad and Ventersburg. These *dorps*, as you call them if you don't live there - it's rather an impolite term, I gather - follow a fairly regular pattern. A dusty main street, crossed at right angles by smaller streets, leads up to the church, the houses and shops being uniformly square and uninteresting with the exception of the farmhouses, which have often the simple but pleasing lines of the old Dutch houses.

At one spot the water was flowing over the road, and while we watched, a large fish flopped its way across, proving it is not just the chicken that has this complex.

Our rule of stopping on the top of a hill stood us in good stead at one camp, for hardly had we finished eating when a terrific storm broke. Lightning flashed and hail lashed round us, and soon the small river from which we had got the water for our tea was a raging torrent fifteen feet deep, which would have carried car, camp and everything away if we had stopped in the more obvious spot nearer the water.

Most of the rivers, dry except in the rainy season, were now flowing freely, although the worst of the flood water was past, and we derived much amusement from fording them, watched by the owners of sleek shiny-looking cars who wouldn't risk it.

We decided to make camp and wait for our German friends, and in the meantime tried to straighten out some of our kit for the entry into Capetown.

Our shirts had long since lost all pretence of being white, and we found that by boiling them with some cheap khaki handkerchiefs we had bought in Jo'burg, they came out quite a good shade of khaki.

After three days' wait, during which we lived mostly on eggs scrambled in the frying pan, we gave the motor cyclists up and continued our journey.

We were now entering the Great Karoo, huge plains covered by small coarse-looking bush some six inches high and apparently dead. We learnt that it provided excellent feed for sheep, and I remembered that I had seen almost the same thing in Queensland and on the lower slopes of the Atlas Mountains in Morocco. Curious little animals [meerkats?] that looked like squirrels dashed about the country and sat up on their haunches to watch us go by. Sand devils, whirling spirals of dust, chased each other across this drear land, promptly falling flat if we tried to photograph one.

Here, too, were the *kopjes*, smooth hills sticking out of the *veldt*, with the peculiar feature that the tops were usually flat, while wind and erosion had worn away the earth at the crests into a sort of battlement effect, so that many of them had the appearance of having a castle on top.

Strange cacti often enhanced the desolation of the scene, which was made even worse by miles and miles of wire fences that seemed to hold the country together, many of them going straight over the tops of the *kopjes* and disappearing into the far horizon.

Rain still continued, and we found the inhabitants of Philippolis and Colesburg overjoyed by the breaking of the drought, many of them stopping us and giving us black tea and dried rusks while they sought information on the rains to the north.

Wet nights caused us to stop under any cover we could find, such as barns, etc., where we often had the company of Cape-coloured boys, usually tramping from farm to farm in search of jobs, who did our cooking for us and called us "Baas". We also frequently met with itinerant musicians, walking along in the dust playing on guitars or battered accordions as they went.

On the day we passed through Hanover, Richmond and Murraysburg, my log records in large letters:- *"Record run; 173 miles and NO PUNCTURES!"*

Lovely nights on the *veldt* after the day's run; first the purple tinge creeping over everything as the sun set, then a new moon trailing across an indigo sky dotted by brilliant stars in which we could pick out the Southern Cross.

To quote direct from my log; *"We have only seen one car all day and we might be in a world unpeopled by human beings besides ourselves, our conversation is hushed, and as I write sitting on the back of the car I can just see the road fading away in the distance among the kopjes, the crescent moon throws curious shadows that people it with imagined forms, and faintly far away I can hear the haunting howl of a jackal. And so to bed."*

Steadily climbing, the *veldt* now being covered with yellow and pink flowers, we were entering the Little Karoo and the great silences, and it was getting much hotter.

*[The Karoo]*

Later the tops of the Hottentot Holland mountains showed up, and here we had to carry both wood and water, neither being obtainable.

One afternoon, the narrow ribbon of the road seemed to climb until it disappeared into what looked like a mountain of snow, but it turned out to be a huge white cloud under which we slipped to drop down into the wonderful Hex River valley.

We were now descending from the vast African plateau on which we had been so long. The road turned and twisted, dropping us thousands of feet. Here it hung over the Hex River, now it dived through a rocky tunnel, the peaks of the mountains rising on either side of us with huge storm clouds hiding their heads, while a terrific wind threatened to hurl us off the road that clung to the sides of the gorge.

Wonderful fruit farms occupied the valley, many of them cultivating the grape, but we were soon out of this enchanted place and climbing again through the wild boulder-strewn pass known as Bains Kloof; then, fifty miles from our destination, we made our last camp.

During the evening a carload of people in full evening dress stopped to ask us the way. The ladies of the party were very interested in our car, and asked where we had come from, and when I told them London, they remarked that they wouldn't have thought we could have done it in a car like that. During the ensuing conversation I gathered they thought I meant East London, which lies on the South African coast.

*Capetown - So near and yet so far!*

The next morning we could see the flat top of Table Mountain, and by eleven o' clock we were rolling through the busy streets of Capetown and up to Rhodes House, the headquarters of the Overseas League, having done over nine thousand miles by car.

# Chapter 11 ~ South Africa

The "Cape Argus" gave us a good write-up, though even now I was not an explorer, the headline simply saying "Tourists from Cairo", but perhaps the members of the League would acclaim us.

*Rhodes House, Capetown*

We prosaically rang the bell of Rhodes House; the lady secretary came to the door and asked:-

"Yes, can I do anything for you?"

In chorus we said;

"We have motored from Vernon House, London, to Rhodes House, Capetown!"

"Really? You must be tired. Come in and have some tea."

During tea we heard of the League's activities in South Africa; then:-

"Well, I'm awfully busy, but you must come again and see us sometime."

And we were outside once more; it was raining and a tyre was down.

We took the kit bag that held all our personal gear and walked off to find a hotel, leaving the car standing in the street. In the evening I again went to the Overseas Club to see if any mail had arrived, and was told that the police had been trying to move the car but could not start it, and had gone to fetch a lorry to tow it away. I should very much have liked to see this operation, which would have been highly entertaining, as I cannot think of any part of the car to which a towrope could be attached that would not have come away as soon as they started pulling. We had intended abandoning it there, then decided it might fetch something, so hurriedly starting it up as only we knew how, the secret being the use of a nail file, we went round to the square and sold it to a junk dealer for fifteen shillings.

John went away to stay with friends, and later joined a motor firm who employed him to lead a batch of drivers who were driving round and round the town on a non-stop run equivalent in distance to the Cape-to-Cairo route as a publicity stunt, while I, having written a few articles for the Press, had sufficient funds to take the train back to Jo'burg. Here the annual Motor Show was on, and I offered my services to the "Star", collecting advertising. They weren't very keen, but let me have a shot at getting it, which I did by walking round the show behind Sir William Morris, as he was then, and pretending I was in his party, and so getting up four pages of dope on British cars.

Castley managed to get me into his office, and for a while all went well, but at the end of the Motor Show, I was told my services were no longer required. I had made friends with most of the motor traders in Jo'burg, so was able to arrange with a firm called Shinwell's to do a reliability run to Durban on a Triumph motor cycle.

Four times I came off on the terribly corrugated road, but eventually got to Durban. The same evening I was sitting on the beach wrestling with the problem of really seeing Africa, my mind idly playing with the most curious ideas; travel meant ships, aeroplanes, cars; rallies - a rally! Why not? South Africa had never had one worth speaking about, and the first South African Motor Rally was planned.

Jo'burg was the place to run it, so although it was then dark, I got the motor cycle out and hared off back on the four hundred odd miles of terrible road, and the following morning presented myself to Mr. Urquhart, the Secretary of the "Argus" group of papers and manager of the "Star", incidentally the paper from which I had just been sacked.

I knew he was keen on the charity run by his paper to send poor children to the seaside, and suggested that we could obtain funds for it through my idea. I then gave him a rough outline of what I had to suggest, making it up as I went along, and somehow tacked on an air rally, gymkhana and ball.

Anyway, it worked, and back I went into Castley's office and started organising. The idea caught on, the motor traders, the Automobile Association and the Publicity Association of Johannesburg backed it to the limit. A call at the Germiston Airport got the arrangements for the air rally moving under the leadership of Mr. Makepeace, the airport manager and Captain Halse, while the two big halls in the Wanderer's Sports Club were booked for the ball.

Checking-in stations were organised all over the country even as far up as Northern Rhodesia, and the Press in each town gave the rally a considerable amount of space. Many of the cars entered did a distance of over two thousand miles, and in my opinion had an even tougher job than those who compete in the Monte Carlo Rally. I was very pleased to see two small British cars come in first and second.

Items for the gymkhana gave me some trouble at first, as I had never seen one, and as I was supposed to be running it, and to know all about it, I had to invent things on the spur of the moment, which in many cases worked out extraordinarily well.

*Motor cycle polo at the Gymkhana [Archie is seated behind smoking his pipe]*

One item which was a great success was a game of motor polo. I purchased eight old T model Fords of the type we had come down on, stripped the bodies off them and put a bumper completely round them and two steel arches over the top where the body should have been, so that when they overturned they would come back onto their wheels again. I think this probably provided the highlight of the show. I personally played in it, and found it a tough and exciting game.

At a given signal the eight cars, four from each end of the field, dashed for the ball in the centre, meeting with a terrific impact. Many of them

85

turned upside down and lay there until someone in their own team rammed them broadside and knocked them back onto their wheels again. With all eight throttles full open and everybody shouting at the tops of their voices, it was absolutely impossible to hear the referee, who was working on the sidelines with an electric motor horn. At one time when the ball was out of play, he came to me and asked me to watch him, so that he could give a signal when the game was at an end, and when I saw him making signs I tried to convey to the others that the game was over, but with no result at all. I took a terrific swipe at the ball with the intention of driving it out of play, and it hit the front protecting loop of my car, bounced into the air, and fell into my hand, and with this I drove through the opposition goal posts amid great applause, convincing everybody that I really did know this game.

These cars were afterwards booked for shows all over the country, and the last I saw of them was at an Agricultural Show, where the game terminated the arena events. The National Anthem was played, and all the drivers were sitting in their cars with their polo sticks upright, when I noticed that one car was on fire and burning furiously, and I could see the agony of indecision on the driver's face as he tried to make up his mind whether he should leap for safety or wait until the end of the anthem.

The air rally was also a great success, the commanding officer of the air force sending down a squadron to give a display, while we had some really excellent stunt artists.

Hardly was the rally over when Sir Alfred Hennessy, President of the R. A. C., Capetown, agreed to my running a rally there under their auspices. With such an ideal situation and the experience I had gained, I was confident of a super show, but unfortunately it was the wrong time of the year and was not the success I had hoped.

However, one bright spot was the opportunity I had to fly over most of South Africa on a publicity tour for the rally.

While in Jo'burg, I had met a charming family, the Netters, the two daughters, Aimee and Madeleine, doing all the cabaret arrangements for me for the motor rally ball. I wanted to spend Christmas with them, and decided to fly there and back. A pilot friend of mine, Bill Williams, offered me a lift, and on a wet drear morning we left Wingfield Aerodrome and immediately started getting altitude to get onto the plateau. We were soon in the clouds but found we could not get a high enough ceiling, and had to take a tortuous course through the higher peaks. There were no landmarks to be seen, and it was only now and again that we were able to catch a glimpse of the ground when the clouds parted for a brief moment. We both kept our eyes open, and I eventually reported to the pilot that I just had seen a village with red roofs, but as he said there wasn't one within a thousand miles of where he thought we were it didn't help much.

Later we got in front of a bad thunderstorm, and with lightning drawing long streaks of fire round us, we were blown along at a terrific pace before coming down for a short break at Kimberley.

*The World's largest hole, Kimberley*

During our stop there, Williams produced some things to suck that he recommended for air-sickness, and although I had done a lot of flying and had never been sick, he made me promise to try one. When we got going again I was tentatively sucking one of these, and when we hit a bump I half-swallowed it, nearly choking myself and making myself sick, while Williams yelled at me to take one of the cures.

The *dorps* below us looked pathetically small from the air, the houses bundling together as though in terror of the vast spaces that surrounded them, while the plains were even more monotonous from the air than they had been when I passed them by road.

The almost white mine-dumps showed up at last, and we landed on the Flying Club aerodrome at Baragwanath. After Christmas, Aimee and I flew down to Durban and back with Rodwell King, the owner of the W. A. C. O. plane in which I had previously flown round Jo'burg, and then I had to go back to Capetown.

The large plane was already on the tarmac when I arrived at the Germiston Airport, but one of the engines refused to start. Someone suggested that we should get out until it got going, as we should be inside for some hours during the flight. Hardly had we done so when the plane caught fire and there was a wild scramble for the fire-extinguishers which were inside the hangar. Each person, as he grabbed one from its bracket, started it going, so that as they ran to the fire they covered each other with the white foam of the extinguishing fluid.

I had gone to the telephone and got onto the Press with what may rightly be described as some hot news, and when I came out of the box the fire had been put out, but the machine was badly damaged and we had to leave in a reserve plane.

Back over the *veldt* again, then dropping down from the plateau, which seemed to be almost slower than when we had done it by car, though the spectacle was even more wonderful, the huge peaks appearing to push themselves up as we floated down towards our landing ground. Studying the country one realised faintly what a superb effort the old *Voortrekkers* had made when they climbed through these mountains with no roads and their sturdy oxen as their only motive power.

The rally over, the itch to be moving again was strong. John was still in Capetown, and I suggested a trip up to Laurenco Marques, Portuguese East Africa. He was for it, and as I had a bit of cash in hand, arrangements were quickly made.

Our transport was a Darracq, ancient but in good condition, and John was of the opinion that if it ever got to the top of Sir Lowry's Pass it would do the trip.

*The Darracq near Capetown*

Our route had been planned to take us along the coast, and the Press photographers came down to get photographs of our start. They were unduly optimistic, for the magneto managed to go phut at the crucial moment and it took us another day to fix it.

Passing through the beautiful mountain country in the south-eastern part of South Africa, we ambled along the shores of the Indian Ocean bathing and camping. At Swellendam the rubber coupling of the magneto gave out and we had to effect a repair by taking a cast of it in plaster of paris and making a new one of lead. Otherwise all was well.

My idea to do some writing for publication in the bigger towns, such as Port Elizabeth, East London, Durban, etc., was O.K., but payment seldom covered the necessary inspiration, so that our capital was fast fading away. However, I had hopes of running a rally or something of that sort at Laurenco Marques, and had already drawn up a rough programme for an aquatic carnival, and in the meantime we were thoroughly enjoying ourselves in probably the finest climate in the world and amongst scenery which has few equals.

A doctor I met at a place on the coast told me that it was one of the most healthy spots one could find. I asked him why he elected to practice in so healthy a place and he pointed out that everyone knew it was good, with the result that invalids came from everywhere to live there and he was getting a wonderful reputation for his cures.

We were merely ambling, and if you will look at a guide-book you will see why. Gouna Forest to Knysna, Lottering Forest and Storms River to Assegaibusch, the range of the Outinigua Mountains, petering out into small hills as we went northward, hilly country once more and up onto the high *veldt*, over the Kei River and into the Transkei, through Umtata, Flagstaff and into the more primitive country of the saffron-cloaked Xosa natives, who seem to preface every word with a click of the tongue; through the heavily wooded country round the Izotsta River, where trees blossomed in bursts of brilliant red, down again to Umkomaas, and into Durban, a route that only a madman would have hurried through.

At Durban I broached the idea of a rally and got as far as a meeting with the town councillors, A. A. and Publicity Association at the Town Hall, but could not get them going, as they said that during the season so many visitors came to Durban anyway that there would not be accommodation for more.

We were told we couldn't get into Portuguese East Africa [Mozambique] without permits, but I had heard that story too often about other countries to let it worry me, and we were soon pushing our way through the mountains that form the basin of the Tugela River, occasionally needing a helping shove from friendly natives, especially when we left the valley with its winding river.

Rain was making heavy going of the earth roads, while I had to wade through the Black and White Umfolosi Rivers ahead of the car, picking out the best track in the swirling waters.

At Gollel we met a car whose occupants said they had turned back as it was impossible to cross the Usutu River. When we got there we found another car stuck in the middle, and it had been there all night, but the water had gone down quite a lot. We got over by travelling fast, doing some marvellous skids in the mud, and once over and on firm ground we were able to haul the other car out.

We often turned right round on the greasy mud roads, and we crossed the Pongola River in almost a cloud-burst, but things improved as the road began to climb into the mountain region of Swaziland.

Our only company was a number of high-shelled tortoises, and we had long arguments as to whether they could be eaten; though I was game to try them John said no, and my log records the fact that we lived for three days on twelve eggs and three potatoes.

# Chapter 12 ~ Mozambique ~ Swaziland ~ South Africa

We had no difficulty with the Customs on entering Portuguese East Africa [Mozambique] except for the fact that the Customs officer pinched his finger in one of my trunks and got very annoyed.

At Laurenco Marques, a Mr. Sprackett allowed us to make camp on a waste piece of ground behind his office, and in the evening we wandered round the town, which has a definitely continental atmosphere with its gay square, done in black and white mosaic, which had a cafe at each corner with a radio going at full blast and a bandstand in the middle. Here in the evening, crowds gather to drink coffee and have their shoes cleaned, for to sit for a moment is to invite a swarm of shoeblacks, who flock round soliciting custom.

We had to change some of our last remaining pound notes and found that the lawful rate at the bank was a hundred and eight *escudoes*, while the Indian traders would give a hundred and twenty-five. Needless to say we didn't patronise the banks.

The next day I approached the Powers that Be with my idea of running a show here, and although everybody seemed in favour of the idea, Sprackett warned us that a-manha (to-morrow) was the watchword in that part of the world, and there was no hope of getting a written reply for at least a fortnight. As we couldn't live that long we decided to return to Jo'burg.

After protracted arguments with a one-eyed Indian storekeeper, who thought we had entirely the wrong idea, and that he should be doing us down and not we him, we left with enough petrol and oil to get us to Jo'burg, a dozen eggs, one loaf and ten shillings.

To save any arguments, we crossed the borders at night, and made camp in time to watch a great fight among a troupe of baboons before turning in.

It had been suggested that we should find it worth our while to visit one of the native communities in Swaziland, so went over to the village known as the Queen's Kraal. The Prime Minister or Witch Doctor, or whatever he was, invited us to visit the queen, whose name sounded to me like "SheBoozer". Going into the *kraal*, or village, we found a huge but intelligent-looking native woman sitting on the hard earth outside the largest of the huts. Ceremonial gourds of native beer were offered to us, and having blown the ash and floating refuse away from the brim, we drank deep and found it good.

This part of the country is supposed to be the scene in which some of Rider Haggard's books are laid, and I tried to check up through our Grand Vizier, who spoke a curious English.

He pointed out a peculiar rock known as Execution Rock, which rose in a long slope and then on the other side dropped sheer, except for a small ledge, and told us with pride that the defeated Impis, commanded to commit suicide, marched in formation up the slope and without breaking their ranks went to their death over the edge. The small ledge was, I gathered, a jumping-off place for ladies who had incurred the royal displeasure, as they could not be honoured by being allowed to jump from the warriors' leap. Sort of "half-way for ladies".

*[Execution Rock, Swaziland]*

We struck the rain and mud again, and at Oshoek, on the other Swaziland frontier, the mud was so thick that we could not follow the road, which ran between two banks, some four feet in height, and formed a sort of river bed. I went ahead on foot to see if we could find a way round, and having gone some distance, saw a horseman leap off one of the banks into the road, followed shortly afterwards by our car, which came down with a terrific crash. It seemed that John had followed the horseman over a drier route, and that leap was its last effort, for it refused to go again.

The chap who kept the store there told us we could "mook in" with him, then added that he would have to charge us something. We explained our almost complete penury, whereat he went inside and slammed the door, so we slept that night in his barn among the ploughs and other merchandise.

In the morning we found the crown wheel of the car was stripped, so when a chap with a rich Lancashire accent turned up and offered us a lift into Jo'burg, we gladly accepted. He had been inspecting a gold claim that had been offered to him by two prospectors who were with him, one being frightfully deaf and the other so ill that I expected him to pass out at any moment. We all crowded into the small Rover car and away we went in the mud. Our host proved to be one of the worst drivers I have ever come across, but a great sportsman.

Peering through the bespattered windscreen, he would say, "Ee, lad, theersa bludy big 'ole, Ah moost miss that 'un" and then with a shattering crash we would go into it, whereupon he would beam at us and say "Ee, Ah was right; that were a bludy big 'ole, that were."

After Kinross, the car ran out of petrol, and we were told, "Next village's not sa far; let's poosh it." Having pushed for about three miles we were overtaken by another car, and were told we only had forty-three miles further to go, and the occupants suggested that one of us should go in with them for more juice.

I was elected, and when we reached the village I had some difficulty in breaking up a poker-party before I could procure some petrol. Having at last got it, the only transport I could find to take me back was a moth-eaten mule. I slung the two-gallon petrol tins over my shoulder on a piece of rope, mounted the brute and set off. All went well until I topped the rise within sight of the stranded party, when, after the manner of its kind, it decided it had gone far enough, and it was not until I hung the tins over its stern that it broke into a trot, my companions stopping it when it reached them. I didn't fancy riding back on it, so we tied it to the back of the car, and although I expected trouble it followed us at a steady trot.

After many vicissitudes, we got back to Jo'burg, where John, deciding that I wasn't safe to know, took a job.

In Jo'burg I lived in luxury with my very good friends, the Netters, at their wonderful home on the outskirts of the town, enjoying the impressive contrast from life on safari, lounging on their sun-bathed *stoep* with native servants to bring meals, wandering in the glorious grounds with the charming daughters, and, luxury of luxuries after muddy rivers, there was a peacock-tiled bath let into the floor of one of the bathrooms in which I wallowed for an unconscionable time every day, only being brought out by shrieks from the rest of the household that it was their turn.

Mr. Netter was an ex-Government Inspector of mines, and I gladly accepted an invitation to visit one of the deepest mines with him. Running out along the Rand between the huge dumps with their crests hidden in clouds of fine dust, we pulled through the large entrance gates and parked the car close to the great whirling wheels that lowered the cages down the shaft.

I had never been down a mine before, and I was rather surprised when we were given oilskins and sou'westers, but I soon learnt the reason when we got into the cage-like affair for the first descent into the bowels of the earth, for water spattered down on us as we went down.

We dropped at an ever-increasing speed for I believe four thousand feet, and it was only when we came to a halt that my inside seemed to catch up with me. Small acetylene lamps were given to each of us, and we set off between huge blocks of whirling machinery, walking through endless corridors of what seemed to be solid rock, water flowing along beside us in many places.

We then came to a spot where enormous buckets (I believe they are known as skips) disappeared down a hole. Our guide must have given some kind of signal, for they stopped long enough for us to get into them.

I was told that the best way to travel was to wedge oneself across the top of the skip with the back braced against one side and the feet against the other, and these instructions I tried to follow, at the same time balancing my lamp, which threatened to set fire to me at any moment.

Someone must have given another signal, for off we shot, for some time running at a steep angle; then there was a jolt and the angle was increased sharply. My complicated attitude could not have been the right one after all, for, in spite of all my scrambling to regain balance, I landed with a dull splosh in the wet mud at the bottom of the skip, and sat on my lamp. Trying to stand up in the darkness proved hopeless, for every time I thought I had got set, the angle changed, and splosh! I went again.

At last we stopped and a voice hailed me. I made gurgling sounds from the depths, and someone gave me a hand out and then told me we had dropped another four thousand three hundred feet.

The heat was terrific, and I could hardly see for the condensation on my glasses, but stumbled on after the party with my lamp roaring like a blowtorch, as I had turned it up too high when relighting it. Every time the party got to the face, or end of the tunnel, which they were inspecting, I was so far behind that they were just turning back when I caught up with them, so that I only had glimpses of the giant pneumatic drills and the shining bodies of the natives who worked them before we were off somewhere else.

Coming to a place that was more open than the tunnels we had been in, the party stopped to discuss something or other, when, with a loud bang, pieces of rock started flying off the wall. It didn't look too good to me, but I was informed casually that it was just a rockburst due to the terrific pressure at this depth. Someone was called up and started picking at the wall, dodging pieces of rock as they flew off, and we left them to it.

It seemed that we were to go still further down, this time through what I learnt was called a *stope*, which appeared like a huge slit in a letter box, the height being I should say just under three feet. The others climbed in and down the steep angle with practised ease, myself a bad last, for if I went on my back I couldn't hold the lamp, and if I sat up I banged my head, and if I went stern first - my behind kept getting jammed on rough pieces of the roof. Furthermore, I didn't particularly like the thought of the tons of earth above me and the rockburst we had seen. I slid the last part at a terrific rate, ending up by sitting on my lamp and putting it out again.

I could see the lights of the rest of the party going down another tunnel, and I groped after them in a cloud of acetylene gas from my lamp, which I lighted from one of the others as I caught them up. Another shaft descended from this point, and I was very relieved to hear that we were not going down this, but were returning to the surface.

# Chapter 13 ~ South Africa ~ Lesotho ~ Zimbabwe

All this was not getting me any nearer the heart of Africa, so I started to make plans for my return journey northward. I had given several broadcasts in Capetown, Durban and Johannesburg, and through these got in touch with Zeederberg's Travel Agency, who had an enquiry for a safari northward, and they put me in touch with Professor Lusk Webster, who proved to be a physicist.

He told me that he was interested in the magnetic survey of the Great Rift Valley, but of more interest to me was the fact that he wanted to go back through Central Africa by road, and was prepared to pay a reasonable fare.

I had to get hold of something good for a trip like this, and paid quite a high price for a well-known make of British car.

The agent for this car had been interested in the Cape-to-Cairo run of Court Treatt. [This was the first expedition to drive a motor vehicle from Capetown to Cairo. Six people, headed by Court Treatt, set off on 13th September 1924 and reached Cairo on 24th January 1926, some sixteen months later, covering 12,732 miles.] He promised to have everything ready for me to set off by a certain date, saying that he knew perfectly well what alterations and equipment I would require.

When I went to collect the car, the water pump was off, both doors, and a few more odd pieces. Next day, in response to my frantic demands for speed, they had got these on, but had taken off the carburettor and lost the starting handle. On the third day all was ready.

As Webster wanted to be one of those few who have done a Cape-to-Cairo run, we had first to go to the Cape, a thousand miles in the wrong direction, and presently I was again passing over monotonous brown *veldt* with only the bright green crops round villages to relieve the eye.

Webster, although quite a young chap, carried a lot of surplus weight. He appeared to be a cheerful bloke, though rather apt to go into deep thoughtful silences, from which he would emerge with the useful information that in so many miles our pistons would have travelled umpteen times up and down, and other obscure calculations which accorded ill with his request to be called Bill.

By this time you will have come to the definite conclusion that I consider no-one except myself knows anything about safari work, and although I must admit this attitude was possibly very trying to my many partners, I usually had considerably more experience than they had in this work.

At Parys, Webster had his first experience at camping. The spot we had chosen was rather beautiful, next to a small river overshadowed with weeping willow. We turned in early and were awakened next morning by a milk boy delivering milk, followed by the baker, which I am afraid gave my partner wrong ideas of the comforts of camp life.

The next day we had our first puncture and found great difficulty in changing the wheel, as the jack we had been given was far too small and would not lift the car sufficiently. This happened very shortly after Webster took over the driving. But I'm not blaming Webster!

Anyway, even if he was unlucky with tyres, my log records that he was "not a bad lad, having passed no rude remarks about my cooking."

The roads were good if we travelled at forty miles an hour, but at any speed under that, the corrugations shook us up badly, while the high wind made things rather unpleasant. That night was bitterly cold, there being 13° of frost, the next morning the car and tent were thick with white hoar-frost, so that the morning leap out of bed somehow lost some of its verve.

Bloemfontein proved to be only a few miles from camp, and a prolonged stay was made in a comfortable hotel there while new tyres were fitted to the rear wheels and a new jack etc. purchased. The town impressed me as being very well-kept, the shops showing up to much better advantage than in Jo'burg.

The country beyond here was badly stricken with drought, and dead sheep lay everywhere. We also saw the dried body of a donkey still standing where it had been caught in the barbed wire as it made for the river.

I developed a spot of fever, and Webster took over the wheel again, and, strange to relate, collected a puncture in one of our new tyres. Not that I'm blaming Webster!

The Zwart Bergen mountains, when we reached them, were covered with snow and enveloped in stormclouds. Rain caught us in the Hex River valley, while every rock in Bains Kloof acted as the brink of a miniature waterfall. Capetown was as bad as Windy Wellington in New Zealand, the wind dashing the rain along the streets and making things very dreary.

While in Capetown I received a cable from the Standard Motor Company, offering to put one of their cars at my disposal. This sounded very nice, but nothing ever came of it, for having cabled back my thanks I got another cable from the Managing Director saying that the car would be at my disposal - in England.

Webster decided to fly to Grahamstown to see friends of his, and I was to pick him up there several days later.

I stopped for a few days with friends in Capetown, spending quite a lot of time with the Danish and Swedish skippers of the whaling fleet which was then in port. I had an invitation to go on a voyage with them, and should very much have liked to accept, but I had contracted to go north instead of south, so had to refuse.

I went on board one of the whalers as it lay alongside, and the skipper, who was also the gunner, took me on an interesting tour of his ship. From the bridge a narrow gangway led to the harpoon gun forward, and he explained to me that this fired an explosive harpoon weighing a hundred and ninety-two pounds. A series of very powerful springs took up the recoil of the gun and the strike, also easing the shock of the whale in its mad plunging. A winch then brought the whale alongside, air was pumped into the carcass, and it was left for the mother ship to pick it up.

He told me that in the last season of six months his ship alone had got one hundred and eighty-two whales, while the season before he had killed two hundred and sixty.

Capetown in the rains richly deserves its name of Sleepy Hollow; everything seems to go dormant until the fine weather comes along again. At the broadcasting station, which was then over a music shop, I found nearly all the staff sitting round a fire having tea, while a large barefooted native carried gramophone records from the selection committee round the fire and put them on the machine, walking about with exaggeratedly high steps to prove he was not making a noise.

In a thirty-four mile run from Capetown, which is fifteen feet above sea level, I climbed one thousand four hundred feet through Sir Lowry's Pass through heavily wooded country, the dark pines looking splendid against the snow-covered peaks. At Bot River the morning was so cold that I lit the petrol stove inside the tent. With numbed fingers I managed to knock it over, and nearly set fire to the tent and the car.

The route was through nearly the same country as I had covered with the Darracq, down through Phantom Pass, Real House, Perseverance, Nature Valley, and on to Port Elizabeth, then through the Tsitsikama Forest, where rain had turned the roads into quagmires of mud which had been ploughed up by the timber haulers.

An old Boer farmer joined me at one camp. Bringing his train of oxen round in a masterly fashion, he soon had his huge Capecart in position for the night. The oxen outspanned, he brought chickens and pigs from under the cover of the cart, set up a large tripod, and presently had a vast black pot bubbling over the fire.

He spoke no English at all, so our conversation was limited. We exchanged pipefulls of tobacco, I finding his poisonous while he, I think, found mine a pansy mixture in comparison to his own.

During the night I was awakened by a snuffling noise at the flap of the tent, and looking up I saw the most curious animal gazing at me. Two small eyes glittered on either side of a long snout, and the really strange thing about it was that it had crossed horns close to its head, and two other pairs on either side of its face. Having stared at each other with mutual distrust for a moment, I threw a boot at it. The response was a definitely pig-like grunt, and the light of the electric torch revealed it was one of my camping partner's pigs with a triangle of sticks tied round its neck to prevent it from going off into the forest.

Webster was ready when I got to Grahamstown, and the following morning, having been wakened by a melodious chime of bells from the church, he borrowed the car to pay a visit to the University and in turning managed to buckle the exhaust pipe up on the kerb. Not that I'm blaming Webster.

When we had straightened out this damage, we went off through scenery which is impossible to describe successfully, and even the camera cannot record its undoubted fascination. It is so endless, so vast, so much the same and yet so different. The stretches of *veldt* - stone and boulder-strewn plains - mountains fading away in a blue haze in the distance - the change from almost white sand through all ranges of brown to a deep red - must be seen if you want to discover the lure of this part of South Africa.

The Katsberg mountains gave us our first change, as we travelled on a road that curved and twisted through bright green foliage with a towering wall of rock on the one side and a sheer drop on the other. As we gained height, we could see the road over which we had come looking like a faint scratch across the *veldt*.

Presently we entered Basutuland [Lesotho], where wild hills, split in half or gashed by landslides assumed fantastic shapes, while the rivers had worn sheer canyons thirty feet of more deep that gashed the plains.

Wild-looking Basutu natives, rather like Mexican *vaqueros* in their bright blankets, worn by putting the head through a hole cut in the centre, dashed about on ragged ponies or lounged round the villages that nestled on the slopes of nearly every hill.

The return run to Jo'burg was made without incident and was chiefly notable for the intense cold, which inspired a line in my log to the effect that, "Africa is a cold country where the sun is hot", a description which can be applied to nearly every part of it.

I had to wait a few days for Webster, who was stopping with friends here, so I made plans for a quick dash up to Swaziland to rescue the Darracq, as I have a distaste for leaving a car that has served me well to rot in the bush. A friend of the Netters, one Captain Sharpe, who was going through to Swaziland, suggested that I might like to come with him, and offered to tow the car from where I had left it.

His car was a prehistoric Rugby, but he had great faith in it, so we set off, making a fast run to Lake Chrisse, round which were curious circular water-holes in which the water changed its levels at certain times. Although I have no scientific grounds for thinking so, I believe oil will one day be found in this district.

Sharpe was a most interesting companion and explained to me, as we travelled, the geological features of the country.

We found that my car had been pushed down a slope into a shed, so we fixed the tow rope and the Rugby pulled it up with ease, much to Sharpe's delight. Forgetting that his car had no brakes, he got out at the top to see if the rope was holding; the Rugby ran backwards and I had to let my brakes go in an effort to avoid a collision, so that both cars ran back with a crash into the shed but luckily did no damage.

The first really steep hill proved too much for the Rugby with the added weight of my car, but I managed to get a team of forty oxen and with these I slowly got to the top, behind the long cracking whips and the cries of "Arno" from the drivers.

M'babane hill we took at speed, and as we slowed down, I jumped out and ran beside my car to lighten the load. Halfway up we were doing well, when Sharpe missed his gears and both cars started to run backwards. I made a flying leap into the front seat of mine and swung into the rock wall at one side of the road. Sharpe was still going backwards towards the other side of the road and the big drop to the valley below; fortunately the towrope held just as he got to the edge, but we could not move until some boys arrived and hauled us up. When we eventually reached M'babane I sold the car for one pound.

When I returned to Jo'burg, I decided to sell the car in which Webster and I had been travelling, and this I soon managed to do by hanging round the Stock Exchange and getting in touch with a chap who had just made a nice profit on the fluctuating gold share market.

I made up my mind to buy another British car, and as the Austin had a name for reliability while the firm was a large one and might be interested in the safari on my return, I obeyed the injunction in the firm's slogan and invested in an Austin, one of the twenty horsepower models, and then had extra tanks for water and petrol fitted.

Off northward on the all-red route once more, to find it very dusty. Just past Warmbaths, we camped near a ramshackle hut where a white man lived who had "gone native". This term usually means little more than that he has married a native woman and has become shiftless and dirty, which is a slander on some of the fine African natives.

I walked over in the evening to have a talk with this man, and he told me that a tiger was doing a great deal of damage in the district, and that a reward was offered to anyone who could shoot it. I suggested that he meant a leopard, whereat he flew into a rage and said that he had lived in Africa all his life and knew the difference between a leopard and a tiger.

He also told me that some of the Europeans from the town had tried to play jokes on him by imitating the growls of an animal, doing it so well that he had let them have it with a shotgun and seriously damaged the pants of one of the jokers.

After Potgietersrust, we left the main road to visit a friend of mine who was cultivating gumtrees at a place called Devil's Kloof. This seems to me an ideal life spent in an excellent climate and reasonably profitable.

We were told that six million eight hundred thousand tons had gone underground in the Rand mines for timbering alone, that the trees grow just over a foot a month, they can be cut after five years, when two stems grow from the butt, and a cold is unknown while working in the eucalyptus-laden air. It sounds fine, but I suspect there is a catch in it somewhere.

The roads we were travelling on were not marked on any maps, though they were reasonably good and took us through marvellous mountain scenery. Many of the trees had flowers like peach-blossom, while others were a delicate shade of mauve or brilliant red. These trees had no leaves, the only greenery being supplied by huge cacti. There was no game, but once we thought we saw a rabbit.

We passed through Wylie's Poort, the towering walls of rock on either side being covered with what looked like bright yellow or green moss, then descended several thousand feet and came back into the area of the baobab trees that I mentioned having seen on the journey southward. In fact I discovered that this was a baobab tree reserve, though I have no idea why they reserve them.

Camp at night was pleasant but often cold, and as there was a new moon we ran through the night on two occasions, so that we made excellent time to the Limpopo River and were soon out of South Africa again. At the border the car had to be run through a shallow dip full of disinfectant, while we were made to wash our hands and the soles of our shoes, this being an alleged preventative of the carrying of cattle disease. We were told that we could not take through with us the large supply of fruit we had bought, so we solemnly sat down just outside the borderline and consumed the lot, just to spite the border guards who probably expected it to given to them.

Almost immediately after the crossing into Southern Rhodesia [Zimbabwe] we saw game, first a few buck, then ostriches, a small leopard which leapt away from almost under the wheels of the car, then a herd of kudu and another of zebra, also some strange birds that I have never seen before.

Our route twisted about to avoid huge granite mounds hundreds of feet in height. I believe they are called the Gupuro Mountains. Trees were perched on some of these small mounds, their roots often splitting the granite, though I cannot imagine how they lived, and the valleys were studded with pygmy baobab trees that carried pink and red flowers. There were also a few mahogany trees.

Our objective was the Zimbabwe Ruins, whose origin still seems to be under dispute. They are built on one of the granite outcrops I have described, one of them, the Acropolis, being a series of walls built with square blocks about eight by eight by four inches. Steps some four of five inches deep lead up through the passages that are not more than thirty inches wide, and in my opinion, which is not worth much, it was built as a fortified post by local native labour, probably for Hausa traders from the north, who used it as a clearing station for the coast or the lakes. I believe some authoritative persons have attributed it to an unknown race and others to the Egyptians, and have estimated that it was built about BC 4000 [The date is now thought to be 1000 AD, the civilisation flourishing until 1600 AD]. The whole place, including the temple etc., was much smaller than I had been led to believe, and we did not spend more than a day there, but continued on into Mashonaland, then turned back towards the all-red route and into Matabeleland.

We made an excellent camp among the tumbled rocks of the Matopos and paid a visit to the grave of Cecil Rhodes. I have never seen anything so simple and so impressive. Imagine a huge bold granite rock with some terrific boulders balanced on its crest. Among these, almost flush with the surface, is a simple bronze plate engraved with "Here lies Cecil John Rhodes".

*[The grave of Cecil Rhodes]*

Outside the enclosure made by the boulders, lies Leander Starr Jameson, and in the far corner was a memorial to Major Allan Wilson and his men who fell at Shangani River in 1893. An inscription on the memorial (which I believe no longer exists) read, "Not one survived".

While we were there the wind swept across the hills almost with gale force, sighing as it rushed through the rocks. Turning from the memorials, the indescribable hills and valleys of World's View, scattered with fantastically shaped boulders piled one on top of another, stretched away on all sides and seemed to protect this spot which is reserved for those who deserved well of their country.

The recent rises in the price of gold had produced activity everywhere, and we saw many one-man gold mines mounted with crude overhead gear, all hard at work. Otherwise the country was monotonous in the extreme, one or two lone buck being the only other life we saw, with the exception of a very large anteater, a most peculiar animal like a large pig, but with a big heavy tail and a curious head. I think it must have eaten an ant that didn't agree with it, as it allowed me to come right up to it and I had to stir it with my foot to make it move, so that I could get an action cinematograph picture of it.

Drought conditions made travelling rather unpleasant, and by contrast, my old camp near the Victoria Falls was one to be remembered. We spent a few days there exploring it more thoroughly than on my previous visit, finding among other things the curious imprint in the solid rock of what looked like a woman's bare foot, which is known as Eve's Footprint.

# Chapter 14 ~ Zambia ~ Malawi ~ Tanzania ~ Kenya

Crossing the border into Northern Rhodesia [Zambia], the only difficulty experienced with the authorities was over a large-sized revolver my companion had. He was told he would have to get permission to carry it and would also have to pay for the licence. He decided it wasn't worth it if he had to go through all these formalities, and told them he would present it to them. They then discovered they were not authorised to take it, and eventually suggested that it had better be put under the seat of the car and forgotten, and this procedure was repeated at each frontier we crossed.

On arrival at Lusaka, we found that the town had grown out of all recognition since my last visit. There were now three hotels, and the day before we arrived, a bank had been opened, while the Government staff and Post Office were still moving into their new buildings.

We decided to make a tour from here out to Lake Nyasa, and I had some difficulty in getting permission to use the new road that was still under construction, and was warned that we might not be able to cross the Loangwa River, also that wild elephant were plentiful.

The road was in [a] frightful condition and seldom allowed us to travel at more than twelve miles an hour. Heavy woodlands shut out the view on both sides, while the few level spaces were covered with elephant grass, some of it over twelve feet high. One or two native villages were passed, but there were very few natives about, and we found that most of them were working on the huge new bridge that was being built over the river.

As we had been warned, one of the new bridge spans had not been completed, and the only ferry I could find was the one that Court Treatt had used. This was merely a light shell, made of canvas stretched over wood, that acted as a roof for one of his cars, but was built specially for conversion to a ferry. However, I believed it had proved unsatisfactory, and he had left it behind when he had crossed the river at a point higher up and it had afterwards been brought down to this spot.

We camped for the rest of the day, planning to cross the next morning, and rather regretted the decision when the mosquitoes descended on the camp at sundown. There was some compensation in listening to the chant of the native bridge gang who were camped below us. Their voices rose and fell on the still evening air, the leader seeming to ask a question to which the rest would sing a response.

Several small native boys were pressed into service and I sent them off to the river to fetch water for us, giving them basins, pots and bottles to fetch it in. They came clambering up the bank with these utensils, full of water, balanced on their heads, and lined up in a row while I took them, and they were most amused when I hung a canvas bucket on a branch and sat down close to it, for the branch broke off and the bucket descended on me, soaking me thoroughly.

In the morning I ran the car down the steep slope onto the river bed and then a number of natives, lent to us by the bridge construction superintendent, pulled us along until we could load onto our ferry, which was a ticklish proceeding. The car had to be completely unloaded, and when we got afloat we only had two inches free, so that any movement would have tipped us into the deep and fast-flowing water.

I had dropped the hood of the car so that it should not catch the wind, and this disclosed a mascot that had been given to me, a woolly monkey. The boys who were carefully poling us over, saw this and were so intrigued that they let us sweep down on the current. They seemed to think it was my special Ju-Ju and treated it with marked signs of respect.

Webster brought our kit over in a fleet of dugouts and we got onto the road again, after handing out *bonsalla* which is the local word for a tip.

One evening was spent with the White Fathers at one of the huge missions I mentioned before. Our host was a real humourist, who preserved a perfectly grave face until he saw we appreciated his joke and then absolutely boomed with laughter.

When we had agreed to stay the night, he suggested that the car should go under cover, for he said the last time a car had been left outside all night, they had found in the morning that hyenas had eaten all the tyres. I didn't like to doubt the word of a White Father, but credulity reached its breaking point when later he told us that he had been out on circuit and had been sleeping one night on a camp bed in the bush, and, feeling a heavy weight on his chest, had opened his eyes to see, in the rays of the moon, a large snake coiled there. Instead of panicking he thought quickly what he should do, and remembered that if a snake was disturbed it would immediately dash for a hole, so he brought his hands together with a resounding clap, at the same time opening his mouth to the fullest extent, and when the startled snake put its head in, bit it off and killed it.

Having told us this, he went off into fits of laughter in which all the other Fathers joined. Two of these were French Canadians, one Dutch and the other South African.

At Fort Jameson, we got in another supply of stores, eggs being plentiful at thirty-five for a shilling and oranges thirty for a spoonful of salt, and set off to N'dazi Boma, where we stopped with the District Commissioner.

En route we came up behind a number of native women who were ambling along in single file, bearing large baskets of *mealies* [sweet corn] on their heads. The one on the tail of the procession heard the car and turned to look, which caused her to fall; the large basket hit the one in front of her, and then the whole line went down rather like the Totem chorus in "Rose Marie". They seemed to enjoy the joke for they roared with laughter.

At N'dazi Boma I was pressed into service to draw the head of a buffalo, which native craftsmen were to carve on the back of a chair, to be presented to the chief of the tribe which showed most prowess in the sports which were held on the King's birthday. Having made some kind of job on this, I went round on a conducted tour of inspection, visiting the native prison and being duly impressed with the new twenty foot deep latrines which were being dug and which seemed to be the District Commissioner's special pride.

We then walked over to the native village where he was encouraging the revival of iron-smelting, which was almost a lost art. He had got together the old greybeards who remembered how it was done, and they constructed a conical tower about eleven feet high built of antheap and reinforced with green sticks. Laterite [red clay soil] was placed in the top section and a fire lit in the bottom into which the iron was melted, being cleared of the ash afterwards. I was told that the inexplicable thing was, that no iron could be extracted unless the witch doctor said his spells and dropped "medicine" into the top.

Crossing the border into Nyasaland [Malawi], we were stopped by an official who told us in a most peremptory tone that we should have to comply with the usual formalities before being allowed into the country. I got all our papers out of the car and followed him to his house. When we got inside, he barked the solitary word, "Gin?" at us, and having fulfilled the rites he said, "Well, that's the formalities over; you can go through now."

As we progressed into Nyasaland we found the country thickly populated with natives who had a curious greeting for us; a long-drawn high-pitched yell ending in a warble made by moving the tongue rapidly between pursed lips. Most of them were leading the local breed of short haired dogs, whose distinctive feature is that they are incapable of barking.

One day we entered a veritable fairyland forest. All the trees were festooned with a long green flowing growth, rather like seaweed, that streamed from every branch, some of it over two feet in length. A troupe of baboons chased each other through the glades as we approached, dancing about from one shadow to another. Lying full length in the shade on the road were two magnificent leopards. Webster already had the camera out, so I inched up to them and managed to stall the engine a few feet away, whereupon they slowly got up and walked off into the forest.

Later we had a meal at Mzimba where we were told that the natives were becoming troublesome owing to the increasing power of the witch doctors, who were selling "medicine" which they claimed would prove, when taken, that one was not a witch, and would also prevent one from being bewitched by the white man.

We had now reached Lake Nyasa, and made a wonderful camp on the promontory jutting out into the clear waters of the lake. The District Commissioner, who was on a visiting tour with his wife, sent over an invitation to dinner, which we thoroughly enjoyed. We stopped a few days here, and were his guests for meals, although we slept in the tent. He warned us of the danger from leopards, but we only heard them once or twice.

One of the disputes he had to settle here was between a man who had made a fishing net and the man he had sold it to. When the maker had sold the net, it was necessary for him to tell the net that it now belonged to the new owner, and must catch fish for him, and this the fisherman said the maker had failed to do, so that he was unable to catch fish.

It is very difficult to realise that this vast area of water is all fresh, as the lake is over two hundred and fifty miles long, and there is a story that during the War, a ship captained by an R. N. V. R. [Royal Naval Voluntary Reserve] officer put into port to obtain drinking water.

It was hard to tear ourselves away from this beautiful spot, but it had to be done, so after one last bathe we followed the road that ran parallel with the lake, climbing again until we could see the blue water far below us, then, after Livingstonia Mission, came to an incredible descent on a track that turned and twisted to such an extent that on sixteen of the turns we had to manoeuvre backwards and forwards before we could get round them.

Fifteen miles away on the other side of the lake, we could see the walls of the cliff rising thousands of feet sheer from the water's edge. Down on lake level again, the vegetation became tropical, palms, paw-paw and bananas growing in profusion, as well as the large golden palm-fruit which the elephants shake off and eat, spitting out the stones. While we were threading our way through the trees we heard the popping of a motor cycle and a man caught us up riding a shiny-looking B. S. A. He told us in one breath that his name was Mr. Charles, that his home was in Bournemouth, and that there were sixteen elephants feeding at the lakeside ahead of us and they might cross our path.

Although we kept our eyes open we saw nothing of the elephants. Later a native told us we must have passed them by not more than two hundred yards.

Arriving at Karonga, we went down for a swim and met the District Commissioner and his wife, who asked us to go up to tennis in the afternoon. Charles, who was the forestation officer, an Assistant District Commissioner, the doctor and a Public Works Department chap turned up to form the largest party that had ever been held in this spot, where the lake steamer only calls once a month.

There was one small store here, known as Mandala Stores, an African name given to it by the first natives to trade there, which means "glasses" and was really applied to the first trader, who had worn them. Here we had to make arrangements to hire a very small boat made of iron, as the road went no further. It did not look as though it would hold the car, but it was the only thing there was.

Before leaving in the morning we visited the small cemetery where the graves of both British and Germans who fell during the Great War, are beautifully kept side by side.

Practically the whole station turned out and helped to push the car up planks onto the iron deck of our craft, which had been punted into a small lagoon. At last we were on board and about fifty natives manhandled the barge through the tall reeds and out into the open lake, our hosts of the previous day coming out in small boats to give us a send-off.

Owing to a high wind the lake was quite choppy, and we rolled considerably, but a small sail was hoisted which steadied us a good deal. As there was practically no room left on the deck, Webster and I sat in the car so that the boys could squat along the sides and paddle.

A large black cloud appeared low down on the lake looking like smoke from a ship, and we learnt that it was composed of Kungu fly which individually were no bigger than a pin's head.

About three in the afternoon we made for the shore where the *capita*, or head man, and the twelve boys had food. Unfortunately the wind now dropped, the lake became a smooth sheet of opal green, and the boys had to take long poles, six a side, working to a chant by the *capita* and all joining in the chorus.

We ran well into the night, the boys' voices carrying out over the water. There was no moon, but the stars gave quite a bright light, one planet making a silvery track across the lake. At about nine we ran into a large school of hippopotamus, who swam after the boat, their huge teeth gleaming in the spotlight that I shone on them. The light also woke thousands of waterfowl on the shore, who rose with deafening cries as we passed.

In the early morning we landed at Moya, our destination, and stopped on the sands until daylight, the crew sleeping all round us.

We had great difficulty in getting the car off onto the bank owing to the angle, but eventually we were ready to move off again, "prizee" (a tip) first being given to the crew, and we then passed through vast banana plantations on a very bad track.

The natives had their huts in small clearings and ran out to welcome us as we passed, the women wearing a particularly attractive dress composed of a band of banana leaf round their waists with two long ends which swung between their legs and emphasised their graceful walk, although most of them, especially the older women, would have looked better with their faces lifted, starting from the tummy.

From here we made a beeline for M'beya, which had grown considerably since I passed through exactly two years before on the way south. A splendid road had been built since then, that took us up into the hills through willowy bamboo forests, where a herd of springbok bounded across in front of the car, seeming to float through the air in their huge leaps.

One evening we camped by a river on the other side of which a detachment of the King's African Rifles were also camped, making a pretty scene with their twinkling camp fires. I sat out in the soft warm night watching them and listening to the plaintive notes of the bugles. Webster, however, was not impressed, as they kept him awake, and as far as I could make out, at each call he took another glass of Eno's.

The country as far as Dodoma was uninteresting bush, although there were many species of buck about, and once we saw a giant forest hog. At Dodoma, which was an old slave centre, we were the guests of the geological research people stationed there, and Webster was in his element. Nearly every word in the conversation after dinner ended in "ology" or something technical, while I carried on a more plebeian discussion with our host's wife on the relative merits of beer and stout.

I found that here the natives always buried anyone who died of disease in holes in baobab trees, their idea being to prevent them from contaminating the ground. Another tree was becoming conspicuous as we went north, almost the antithesis of the baobab; it was the euphorbia, or candelabra tree, with practically no trunk but all branches.

We were now running on top of the watershed that divides the Indian Ocean, Atlantic and Mediterranean, and from our altitude we could see plains fading away into the distance on either hand. However, we were still in woody country and saw quite a number of antelope and several hairy-looking apes. We also passed a small lake in which we could see twenty or thirty hippo.

The natives here had much sharper features than those in the south, which showed their consanguinity with the Arabs or northern races. I often wished I had more time to study the tribes, but I had to wait another three years before I made this trip again, when I had more leisure.

One more detour from the all-red route took us across the Serengeti Plains, famous as a hunter's paradise, to the Ngorongoro Crater, the largest known crater in the world, thirty-five miles in circumference, containing a lake, forest, plains, and teeming with all kinds of game. Climbing to the edge of the crater, we had to pass through the clouds, and got so wet that Webster went down with a bad dose of malaria, which cut our visit short.

The Wambulu or Erok native huts were curious affairs, half cave, but with a roof built out in front, covered with earth and grass, which made them very difficult to pick out, and surrounded by a palisade of strong wooden stakes with only one entrance, which could easily be closed, affording protection from the warlike Masai, who were their hereditary enemies. Usually standing outside these dwellings was an earthenware pot some four feet high and very crudely made, presumably to hold their water supply during a siege.

As Webster was feeling pretty rotten, we decided to make a quick run for Arusha, and leaving the lip of the crater we got a glimpse of the active volcano Ol-Doinyo-'l-Engai (The Mountain of God). We disturbed herds of game as we came down to the shores of Lake Manyara, along whose desolate margin huge sand-devils chased each other. The car was running in thick volcanic ash and sent up clouds of dust that followed us.

Near Mount Meru, which juts up out of the plains to seventeen thousand and forty feet, we came across herd after herd of giraffe, who galloped ahead of us with ungainly strides.

Lines of Arusha natives, who ape the Masai in their customs, were heading for the town, the women carrying great bundles of firewood or milk in long-necked gourd bottles, dressed in vile-smelling skins and with their ears pierced and heads shaven. They also encumbered themselves with enormous collars of brass wire and massive armlets and anklets made from ring after ring of thick copper wire. The men plastered their hair with red ochre and wore a few feathers in it. They carried only a long-bladed spear.

Webster went straight to the hotel at Arusha and was in bed for a week, during which I toured about the countryside seeing snow fall and melt again on Meru, and one day taking the car on a terrific climb up the slopes of Kilimanjaro, watched by the Wachagga natives, who sat in front of their beehive-like huts, to where I could see the eternal snow line just ahead of me, towering up to nineteen thousand seven hundred and twenty-seven feet.

*The crater of Kilimanjaro*

110

Webster began to feel fitter and we made a quick run through to Nairobi, passing the astounding natural soda lake at Magadi, which looked like a layer of pink icing sugar.

When we reached Nairobi, Webster decided to fly over to the Seychelle Islands before returning home, and that was the last I saw of him until I met him on top of a bus in Piccadilly nearly two years later.

# Chapter 15 ~ Kenya ~ Uganda

For some months I remained in Nairobi, going out for hunting safaris and writing up brochures for the different companies who conducted safaris for rich tourists, most of whom were American. Many of the safaris were lavishly equipped with special tents, ice-chests, wireless, and often aeroplanes.

While I was there the American Press came out with a strong protest against the catching of lions with fishhooks, and published a photograph showing a lion on the end of a rope. What actually happened was that a well-known American millionaire took a lorry out onto the Serengeti Plains, and having shot a buck, dragged it behind the lorry on a long rope. At one point there were seven lions snarling round the carcass, and he was able to get some fine photographs. The photograph published had been taken when a lion worried the end of the bloodstained rope.

Working in the offices of these companies, I came in touch with the most curious people, who wanted to go hunting. The white hunters who usually conducted the safaris were a fine set of men, and their job was often unenviable, especially when they were in charge of a party who thought that money could purchase everything, and many times I wondered why these people came out there.

I remember two brothers, Americans, who were in the office arranging a safari. They had stipulated that there should be every conceivable comfort in their camps. One brother was apparently paying for everything, which ran well into four figures, while the other brother was doing all the arranging. The white hunter who was listing their requirements asked the man who was paying, and who had sat without saying a word throughout the interview, if the inventory he had made of the necessary camp kit, rifles, etc. was satisfactory, to which he replied, "Say, can I get cold beer on this trip? I can? O.K.!"

Then there was the opposite type, an Indian Army officer who came in for information and then went off with one boy carrying an enamel basin with a leather cover over its top as his sole equipment. He came back with a fine bag, and when I asked him how he got on, especially when it rained, he said, "Oh, fine; when it rained I just took off my clothes and put them in the basin and went naked until it stopped."

Kenya is a beautiful country with a marvellous climate, and I cannot understand why Britishers with sufficient capital do not flock there. Nevertheless the urge to move again, which with me amounts almost to an illness, was strong, so that I was soon planning, with a handsome and irresponsible Swede, to make a safari to the Gold Coast [Ghana].

The car was overhauled, but my newfound friend, taking me on a visit to the aerodrome, to meet some of the R. A. F. [Royal Air Force] who had landed on a long-distance flight, overturned the car and put me in hospital with a badly-damaged leg, which turned septic. At one time there seemed every chance that I should have to have it amputated, but later it took a turn for the better. One of my fellow patients was a police officer who had been shot in the lung by a native arrow. He was, like most of the Kenya police, a large and well-built fellow, and it was ridiculous to see him sitting on the edge of his bed blowing up toy balloons, which he had to do to inflate his lungs and get them working properly again, however I am glad to say he was getting on well when I left after a stay of nearly two months.

During my stay in hospital the Swede had apparently been serenading the daughter of the chief of police one night, doing the thing properly with mandolin and song, which had so incensed her father that he had first fired off his revolver at him and then chased him with a hippo hide whip, and I never saw him again.

While I was convalescing, I met two chaps who wanted to go on a trading expedition among the natives in the Tana River area, and it was arranged that if I would supply the transport they would supply the trade goods, but before I was ready to start one of them dropped out.

The other, Courtney Applin, was a man after my own heart, an ex-B.S.A. policeman, and a fine shot and hunter, and we tuned up for the trip which was to take us almost along the equator and across the centre of Africa.

Before leaving Nairobi, I paid another visit to the game reserve to recuperate, and at camp the first night a lion and three lionesses walked within twenty yards of me, and later in the night a leopard and a cheetah came almost up to the tent itself.

Calling at the resthouse, I met Gig Davison, one of the best organisers of safaris in East Africa, and with him a young woman who was on a visit from Cape Town and wanted to get some game photographs. In the afternoon, Gig took us up very close to a large bull elephant, and from our cover in the short bush we got some excellent photographs. He had warned us to keep well hidden, but to our surprise and dismay the lady stood up and started to change the film in her camera, and we had to beat a hasty retreat as the elephant had seen us.

In the evening we drove out along the road and saw hundreds of antelope. One herd ran ahead of us but kept stopping and making curious hissing noises, then turned and streamed back past the car, and we found there was a cheetah in front, which had turned them. On the way back we saw a number of jackal and hyena, and later two porcupines and a civet cat crossed the road in front of us.

I stayed for a few days in the resthouse, and while there assisted in the damming of a river and the erection of a water-wheel to supply the resthouse with electricity. Our first job was to cut trees to fall across the river, and we then started packing them with stones to form the dam, but during the night elephants came down and removed the trees.

I left Gig to finish the job and returned to Nairobi, as I had promised to rewrite a hunter's talk which was to go over on a special broadcast relay to America. When I listened in to the programme I hardly recognised my script. The talk was preceded by a boy speaking Swahili, and the hunter who was broadcasting the talk spoke in such broad Scots that it was almost unintelligible. I heard later that letters had been received from America saying the programme had come over clearly and they were surprised at how much they had been able to understand of the talk in Swahili on elephants.

*Courtney Applin*

Finally Applin and I pushed off, and here is a direct extract from my log, which shows the kind of country we were in:-

*"Lake Naivasha Camp.*

*Left Nairobi at eight-thirty a.m. and climbed seven thousand feet, when the Great Rift Valley stretched out before us. We then dropped to some five thousand six hundred feet. Rather bumpy. Mount Kenya towering seventeen thousand and forty feet to the north, and the extinct craters of Longonot and Suza to the south, the Rift wall sheer on either side."*

It reads more like a journey by air than a trip in an eleven-year old car. Lake Naivasha, by the way, was the original setting of Rider Haggard's "She".

We were to climb still higher, to an altitude of eight thousand six hundred feet, where, although we were nearly on the equator the nights were bitterly cold.

A camp before Kisumu provided some excitement. I had wandered a little way from the camp to get a better view of the wonderful country, when there was a rustling in the bush and then a pounding of feet, and I turned to find a rhino coming full tilt at me. It was so close that I had no time to think, but took a terrific leap backwards as if I had stood on a heavily charged electric rail and the rhino passed so close that I could have touched it. Luckily it kept going, and by the time I had picked myself up it was nowhere to be seen.

Our route now skirted the Gulf of Kavorondo, where the women of the Kavorondo tribe flocked out to see us, dressed in their multitudinous necklaces, bangles and anklets of brass wire, and brass breastplates.

We made a short stop at Kisumu hospital to have my leg re-dressed and had dinner with one of the sisters. She told us she was just out from home, and although she liked her work she found the natives difficult. That morning she had diagnosed a bad case of pneumonia, and had sent the native to bed with a temperature of 106°, but when the doctor arrived, the patient could not be found. It was discovered later that he had got mixed up with a working party and was happily cleaning the windows. We also met the doctor, who recounted how, when giving the nurses a Christmas dinner, he had instructed the native servants to serve the Christmas pudding with the brandy on fire, with the result that one boy carried in the pudding followed by another with a plate of burning brandy, trying desperately to avoid setting fire to his hands.

Crossing Uganda, Applin's gun kept us well supplied with waterfowl, lesser bustard and guineafowl, which made wonderful eating.

We crossed the bridge above the Rippon Falls, which is where the Nile is born, and made camp for three days on the west side of Lake Victoria, only some sixty yards from the water's edge.

All day the hippo played in front of us, and at night came ashore quite close to the camp. The full moon showed a scene of such unsurpassable beauty that we erected a mosquito net at a point of vantage so that we could sit out under it, but when we got inside we found that the close mesh made it impossible to see anything at all. The ludicrous situation of sitting out on a knoll unable to see a thing struck both of us so forcibly that we burst into shouts of laughter, which startled five or six hippo who had been ashore feeding behind us, causing them to charge for the lake passing within about thirty yards of us, so we hurriedly got back to the tent, where for no reason at all we felt much safer.

While we were at this spot, the Buganda natives brought us many presents of fruit and fish, the latter straight from the lake, where they had caught them from their curious craft whose keel runs out forward to make a kind of false prow to which a bunch of feathers is usually tied.

The country was now changing, and we entered belts of thick forest broken by large swamps covered with papyrus.

While camped on the lake near Entebbe I was reading an English newspaper which gave an account of how Colonel Someone had rescued a maiden from being sacrificed to the sacred crocodile, Lutembe, and, how, having got her from the lakeside, he had dashed to his tent two jumps ahead of the croc and tied up the flap, to hear the reptile crashing its jaws together as it walked round the tent looking for an entrance. As we were near the spot, I thought I would get a native version of the story. A native assured me that Lutembe existed, and asked if I would like to see it. I had to buy some fish, and then the boy walked out to the end of a beached dugout and knocked on its side. A huge crocodile answered the call, took the fish from the boy's hand, looked at me with an obvious grin, slowly closed one eye and returned to deep water.

Again the women visited the camp with presents. Their clothes consisted of swathes of coloured cloth, and they wore no ornaments. Although their faces were quite pleasant, they had most curious figures with a terrific stern over which they draped a loose sash, as if to emphasise it.

Several leopard approached our camp and did not seem to be at all afraid of our fire. One came so close that Applin very nearly fell over it when he went to fetch a log from our woodpile.

We were wakened in the morning by a rousing tattoo, and could not at first make out what was causing it. Then we saw that a heavy rainstorm was slowly approaching and the noise we could hear was made by the large tropical raindrops pattering on the broad leaves of the banana trees and palms.

The rains had now set in, so wherever possible we stopped the night in the resthouses that were generally to be found at the end of each day's run. Usually natives turned up to act as guard, and when I asked one of them what they were guarding us from, he replied he didn't know, but white men always wanted a guard, so they always set one. I had quite a job waking him to give him a tip in the morning before leaving.

We could now see the dim outline of the Congo Mountains ahead of us, and the road started dropping down to Lake Albert, passing on the way a fine statue of an elephant that overlooked the water. It was erected to the memory of Pete Pearson, a famous game warden, who had shot his largest elephant on this spot.

Lower down we stopped with a Public Works official who was occupying the huts which the Duke of Windsor, then Prince of Wales, had used while visiting this part of Uganda.

The official told us that the day before our arrival he had had an American lady visitor, and he had taken her to visit the native king's boma. On arrival there, she had dashed up to the king and grabbed his hand, crying, "Say, chief, I'm real glad to know you!" and the chief, wishing to be polite, had used the only English he knew and said, "Good-bye" which rather defeated her.

Dropping down to the shores of the lake, we found that we should have to wait a few days before we could cross on the Robert Coroydon. This large vessel of eight hundred and sixty tons displacement had been brought up piece by piece on bullock wagons and assembled on the lake, and now they were bringing up a floating dock for it.

We had a most pleasant time with the ship's officers while we were waiting to sail, having some splendid fishing, although we didn't catch any of the three-hundred-pounders which were said to be there.

We were told that salt mining, the oldest industry known in Africa, was carried on round the shores of the lake. The mines are owned by the women of the tribe, who hand them down from mother to daughter. The women choose their husbands and make them work for them.

They have a curious legend that deals with a huge flood that happened "cala cala" (long ago). When the flood water receded, there was little food, and search parties were sent out, and those who first found eggs had all the eggs allotted to them, those who found fish had fish, and so on. Even to this day one section of the tribe will not touch another section's special food.

We were almost sorry when the day came for us to sail away from this lovely spot set among the fragrant frangipani trees, the colourful blood-red acacias and the green palms against the blue of the lake. However, as usual there were drawbacks to the place; a swarm of locusts paid us a visit, and at night an animal or insect that looked rather like a crab would come up out of holes in the ground and set up a shrill whistle that human ears could not stand, and it had to be killed as soon as possible. The place was also overrun with huge lizards looking like small prehistoric dragons some two feet in length; these had dark blue and brown bodies and brilliant orange heads and tails.

Before we left, the Indian community, which is a large one in Uganda, invited us to the celebration of the birth of a son and heir to their head man. As I could speak Hindustani, I was feted with as much whisky as I could manage, so I was nursing a thick head when we set off in the morning.

# Chapter 16 ~ Congo ~ Central African Republic ~ Chad

Two and a half hours later we landed on the Congo shores at Mahagi Port and started the long climb up the escarpment, where the road is reserved on alternate days for up and down traffic.

One travels on the right-hand side of the road in the Congo, and we were asked by the Customs officer if we intended to disregard this and travel on the left, as there was an Englishman farming on this side of the lake who went periodically on the jag, and on these occasions he erected a flag on his car similar to ours and swore that he was in England, and to prove it always travelled on the left.

The natives here were the Acholi, the women's dresses consisting of a very small bunch of leaves in front and a few blades of grass behind - and what a behind! I am sure they would topple over backwards if it were not the huge tummies and pendulous breasts that seemed to keep the balance.

*[Acholi family group]*

118

The roads were excellent, so we made up the time we had wasted waiting for the boat at Butiaba by travelling late, when the car would become a shining mass of fireflies. Ribbon development had set in even here, as we were passing through an endless succession of native houses, whose roofs came right down to ground level.

Camp was made one night in a huge grass hut that had been used by the Martin Johnson film company, and the Wamba natives seemed to think we were another company arriving to film them.

One day we entered a long avenue of palms which led us into the heart of the Ituri forest, and for a hundred and eighty miles the forest was so thick that it was impossible to get off the road to make camp, so that we eventually had to camp on the road. Although we had seen few natives all day, as soon as we stopped we were surrounded by a crowd of them, none of them more than four feet high.

In the evening they brought us presents of huge bananas, ten inches in length, and other fruit, and while there I met Pan and his sister and Old King Cole.

*Old King Cole*
119

Pan was a pygmy three feet high with a milk chocolate complexion, a sharp pointed chin, and long pointed ears. Round his neck he wore the fluffy tail of a monkey, and round his tummy a brilliant strip of cloth. He leapt out from behind a mahogany tree probably a hundred and twenty feet in height and with long graceful bounds came up to me and shook hands. His sister followed him, her hair done in curious ridges, and with the same elfin face and pointed ears. She stood within a few feet of me as I prosaically fried bacon and seemed to be enticing me into the forest with a plaintive little tune played on a peculiar instrument made of steel strips fixed to a piece of wood, which twanged softly as her long fingers caressed them.

Old King Cole was a merry old soul, and he arrived at the head of a large party of small folk who twittered round him as he walked. He wore a basketwork crown in which feathers stood upright, a curious sash encircled his great paunch, and he carried a pipe some three feet long, three spears, and a bow and arrows.

A present of some tobacco for the pipe produced a grin that threatened to remove the top of his head. We had no common language, but by signs I indicated that my lady charmer was *une belle femme*; he seemed to agree, and taking her by the arm indicated that he was making me a present of her.

This was a little embarrassing, so to gain time I sent her off to fetch water for us, which caused our whole audience to go off into peals of laughter.

Not to be outdone in courtesy, I let him hold our spotlight on the end of its lead and then switched it on. There was a deathly hush, but the old man stood his ground, looking as if he held a bomb which he expected to explode at any moment.

Next morning we continued along our road, hemmed in on both sides by the thick forest where tall trees were interlaced with gigantic creepers, the road being alive with millions of butterflies, some of them inches across the wings, and others small brilliant fragments of colour.

In the afternoon, we came to a clearing where a ritual dance was going on. The dancers were even smaller than the natives we had met before and perfectly formed. The centre of the space was occupied by a pygmy drummer who had a wooden drum carved into the shape of a vase with a long handle which went over his shoulder. Three lines of dancers shuffled round in circles, and as we watched, the line composed of older men, many of whom had long beards, shuffled towards the drum and the leader spoke a few words to the drummer, who replied with a tattoo on the drum. Each dancer in turn spoke to the drummer and was answered, while the younger men in one line, and the women in another, shuffled round stamping their feet in the dust.

*Ituri Forest Pygmies - these shy little people are induced by presents of meat, to give us a display of their dancing.*

River after river had to be crossed on ferries made by lashing boards over large dugouts. With the exception of the course of the river, the forest ran on both sides in an unbroken wall. Monkeys swung above our heads and brilliant parrots and other birds skimmed over the car. Chimpanzees scuttled across the road in front of us, and twice we heard the noise of gorilla before we got to Stanleyville and made our camp beside the swift-flowing Congo, a thousand miles from its outlet to the sea.

*The Falls at Stanleyville*

Here, camped under the palms in a temperature well above the hundred mark, we watched the paddle boats chugging up against the current or sliding softly by with it, and as they tied up to the bank close by us we should have not been surprised to hear Paul Robeson [American actor of the time, famed for this role] burst into "Ol' Man River", so much did they look like properties from "Show Boat".

One of our jobs was to act as unofficial mail carriers, and before we left we had quite a bag of mail to deliver en route, including some parcels whose delivery was to introduce us to the sender's friends, who, according to him, would give us a wonderful welcome.

A short stop was made to photograph the large volume of water that dropped some thirty-five feet to form the Stanley Falls, and to watch the natives in their dugouts fishing in the swirling eddies just below.

Then we were off into the forest again, but here the road was lined with huts, the inhabitants being happy, intelligent people, at least, intelligent enough not to work, for we always found them lounging in a sort of central meeting house, lazily watching the sun cross the sky.

Most of the men had their teeth filed to points, and nearly all wore knives. A large wooden drum was usually under a separate roof close to the central hall, and as we passed it would be beaten and we could hear an answering beat from ahead of us.

Applin was having great difficulty in shooting for the pot, as he could not get off the road to hunt, but the natives who usually visited us at night, always brought presents of eggs or fowls, so we did quite well. These natives could imitate monkeys so perfectly that we were often fooled by them, much to their amusement.

Several bad storms made going difficult, and we often ran between two fans of spray sent up by the wheels on either side. We were now going northward again, and were getting out of the Ituri forest and into open country, or country covered with gigantic bamboos.

At Bangassou [Central African Republic], we delivered the parcels that had been entrusted to us, and sure enough we were made much of. Cold beer was brought out, and soon several people came and joined a very merry party. In the morning we were to cross into French Equatorial Africa [French Congo, Gabon, Oubangui-Chari, Chad and French Cameroon], and before leaving went to say good-bye to our friends, when they presented us with a bill for all the beer that we had drunk at the party.

Crossing the river that forms the boundary, the native paddlers first passed round a large pipe, then broke into a loud chant. At the end of each stanza their paddles dipped into the water, while the helmsman did a stamping dance on the flat prow of one of the dugouts and a special drummer kept time.

A limp tricolour hanging in the sweltering heat above a mud fort reminded us that we were in French territory, though we saw no white men. This was perhaps just as well as, now we were in open country, Applin bowled over several antelope for food although we had no licences.

At Fort Sibut we made an addition to our party; a small grey monkey which we named Congo. We bought him from a native for a box of matches and he introduced himself to me by biting off half my finger. We were also offered a beautiful little lion cub, but we could not house him in the car, worse luck.

*Me, Congo and Applin  [Congo the monkey is perched in the middle]*

Although we were getting plenty of violent rainstorms, the heat was terrific, and it was very hard to get any sleep under the stuffy mosquito nets. When we did get off to sleep we were awakened by leopards, which were probably after Congo, our monkey. At the sound of them he used to go off into a gibbering rage, and then get under the nets and dance on our naked bodies, simply twittering with fury.

One night a leopard came right up to the tent. Applin grabbed his rifle, but couldn't get it out of its canvas cover, as it had got wet, so I seized the other end and we had a tug of war to get it out, the leopard snarling at us all the while, and then walking off as soon as we got the rifle clear.

Later in the night, Applin woke me with a frightful yell, and I thought the leopard had come back and got into the tent; however it proved to be a field mouse that had tried to burrow in his ear.

We were now approaching Lake Chad and saw the first horsemen we had seen since leaving Rhodesia, also some fine-looking natives who were much taller than ourselves.

Fort Archambault [now called Sarh], was the headquarters of the Mitrailleurs, Senegalese, and the Marine Gunners, who had now become a mechanised unit. The square was a marvellous sight, as the ground was covered with blood-red blossoms.

In the evening we joined the soldiers in a bar kept by a Greek, where everyone was swallowing vast quantities of Pernod. Once again I was mistaken for a German, and I nearly got into a fight with the crowd, a tough one if ever there was one. Some had wild-looking beards and some had the woolly hair of the Martinique, and all were very tight and imbued with a bitter hatred of anything German.

Having explained that I was English, I was "*mon ami*" for the rest of the evening, especially when we took our turn at buying drinks whose cost worked in a curious sliding scale that got less the more you had.

Continuing next day, the road faded out, but a finely-built native put us onto the right track. His dress was, to say the least of it, odd; a small antelope skin was wrapped tightly round his waist with a short strip passing between his legs from the rear. A hole had been cut in this through which his penis had been inserted and drawn tightly back between his legs, while he was carrying a most strange-looking weapon.

We were finding it increasingly difficult to get food. The natives could only offer us poor-looking rice and onions, so we eventually tried some of their dishes, and thoroughly enjoyed what I think were fried woolly caterpillars, which looked like whitebait and tasted rather like insipid shrimps.

At Fort Lamy we were invited to dine with the French Resident, and I caused some consternation by asking for a bath in the quarters that had been allotted to us. Eventually I was shown a room in which stood a large earthenware jar. The water in the jar was tepid, but it was the coolest I had come across for some time. I had started to bail it over me with a tin dipper, when the mat closing the opening that served for entrance was pushed aside, and a sentry with a fixed bayonet marched in ahead of a string of prisoners who were wearing iron collars and were linked together on a long chain. Having got these lined up along the wall of my bathroom, he presented arms, and with as much dignity as I could muster in my birthday suit, I acknowledged the salute; the prisoners then filled my jar from the pots they carried on their heads, and then, with another salute from the guard, they marched out again.

Twice on the following day we had to cross large rivers, while the track was getting extremely muddy, but the going was made easier for us by an endless strip of coarse grass matting that had been woven by the natives and laid over the more sandy parts to allow the passage of cars.

We had now got back to a more cultured type of native. Flat-topped houses built of dried mud were similar to those in Egypt, while the people had had a far cleaner cut of feature. The men wore loose robes held together by a red or blue girdle, through which was thrust a long sword in an ornate scabbard. They also wore large-crowned straw hats that fitted loosely over the tops of their normal cloth headdresses. These were the dignified Hausa and Fulani, usually mounted and carrying three long spears and a shield and followed by a number of wives, many of them absolutely naked and wearing large ornaments in their lips and two things like horns protruding from their nostrils. Kissing was obviously out in these parts.

# Chapter 17 ~ Chad ~ Cameroon ~ Nigeria

We had now entered French mandated territory in the Cameroons, and were running through bush country, which calls for little description, being the endless small trees that cover most of Africa, but it is all painted with a large brush and the road only cuts a narrow furrow through a vast area. For over a hundred and fifty miles a fire had blackened the country, and then we were back again into the bush.

Rather an amusing incident occurred on this stretch. I was always on the lookout for any rattle or squeak that might develop in the car and liked to trace it and remedy it immediately, so when a high-pitched recurrent squeak was heard, we both listened carefully, but whether we put our heads inside or outside the car the noise sounded somewhere else. This continued for some miles, until I stopped the car and turned off the engine. To our astonishment, the squeak went on, and we found that it was caused by thousands of crickets which were chirruping along the roadside.

The natives en route were a wild-looking lot, and we found some difficulty in camping, as they were often drunk and unpleasant. The rain made us use what resthouses there were, and we usually found that the village goats had somewhat the same idea.

Later the country got even more desolate, being very similar to that in Rhodesia, dry looking scrub and plenty of desert, and here and there terrific outcrops of what I took to be granite, one being especially noticeable, rising from the plains and going straight up for hundreds of feet, looking rather like a stage property to mask the entrance to the largest town under French administration - Maroua.

The mud walls enclosing the houses of the town formed a labyrinth impossible to penetrate without a guide, but there was no lack of these. We soon had small boys clinging to every part of the car and shrilling directions at us.

It was very easy to see that this had formerly been a German colony by the well-built fort-like structures that dominated the town, and were now used for administrative offices.

The manager of the Niger Company, a Mr. Bell, was the only Englishman in the town, and we sat up until two-thirty a.m. talking and then turned in on camp beds in the compound of his house, waking to find the walls swarming with vultures waiting to see if we were really dead.

I was talking to an old native who spoke English, French and German besides his native tongue, and I asked him who he would sooner be ruled by. He admitted that the younger men preferred the British, but said that he himself preferred the Germans, for he said that if anyone did anything wrong, the French made a terrific fuss and punished everybody, the Germans at once punished three or four, very often the wrong ones, but the British investigated so carefully that they found out other things that were wrong, and when they found the original wrongdoer it had taken so long that all had forgotten about it and considered any punishment unjust.

Bell told us that we had little chance of getting into Nigeria, as the rains had ruined the tracks, and any primitive bridges there had been across the rivers, had been washed away, but as the last two days had been dry we might just do it; he had sent his last lorry-load of gum, hides and snakeskins out a few days before.

The first river bed was still dry, and we went down the bank at such an angle that I expected the car to turn over. We then had to dig away the other bank to get out again, a procedure that was repeated three times, working in temperatures of 135°F [57°C]. Even the few natives we saw had bunches of leaves on their heads to act as sunshades.

In spite of large areas of water left by the rain, the rest of the country was dry, and the wind carried clouds of sand and dust, so we were glad to accept the invitation of a fine-looking native mounted on a beautifully caparisoned horse to stop the night at the resthouse in his village.

In the evening, many horsemen arrived and put up a wonderful show in the bed of the dry river, charging at each other with long spears like lances, and only pulling up their horses when they were within a few feet of each other.

A most impressive act was put on for our benefit. We stood on one side of the river bed, and then, with the brilliant hues of a dying sun as a background, the horsemen, with robes flying, charged straight at us and pulled up with the heads of their spears almost touching us. Personally I didn't feel too happy facing the thundering charge of wild horses, and afterwards I said to our host, "What would happen if they couldn't pull up in time?" To which he replied gravely, "That would be terrible; the men would never hold up their heads again."

We had a meal with our host consisting of eggs, millet fried in oil, and what looked like the Arab dish, *Fool Maddamis*, which is composed of small red beans boiled slowly for twenty-four hours in a sealed pot and then recooked in oil or butter before being served.

Soon we crossed the border into Nigeria at Maidugari and ran through uninteresting flat country, which was very sandy in parts as we were now on the fringes of the Sahara. Long strings of complaining camels, usually tied end to end and led by a very small donkey, shuffled along with their loose stride, sending clouds of dust into the air.

Most of the towns we passed had the remains of the old walls still surrounding them, while the majority of the dignified inhabitants wore long swords.

Kano was the largest town we had visited for a long time. Here the tides of busy modern commerce surged against the thirteen-mile wall that still protects the native town. Thirteen ornamented gateways lead inside, and the old slave market still stands alongside Lake Jakara, which supplied the inhabitants with water during the siege.

From Kano we turned almost due south, making for Lagos on the coast. As we travelled along the good but dusty road, we met natives going to market bearing all kinds of merchandise, opalescent pink earthenware pots, firewood, grain, etc.

Then we passed through the great gates with their cowhide doors into Zaria.

*The gates of Azari, Nigeria*

Later we stopped at a small market held under what I took to be a casuarina tree, and attempted to buy eggs. Describing eggs in sign language is not so easy. Applin and I clucked and crowed and flapped our arms for wings and pretended to lay eggs for a long time before we got them, much to the delight of the idlers, a cheerful sort of Rip Van Winkles, who chortled with laughter at our efforts.

At Kaduna, we were told that we should have to take to the railway for some distance. There seemed to be a hazy idea that there was a road but anyway it would be closed owing to the rains.

There was considerable excitement in all the Nigerian towns we passed through, as several of the paramount chiefs were on their way to England, which seemed to necessitate a great many visits from minor chiefs with their retainers, always protected from the sun by coloured umbrellas which were twirled and bobbed as they were carried aloft, making a vivid scene which was enhanced by the many-hued robes of the native police.

Leaving Kaduna, the road almost immediately petered out, but a fair track took us through brilliant green undergrowth, the leaves of which had a glossy sheen like patent leather. The natives we met en route seemed to be very primitive, the women wearing small aprons decorated with cowrie shells. These shells are locally legal tender and represented their dowries. Others had a curious round disc like a small target slung on their behinds.

Most of the bridges had been washed away and those that still remained were in such poor condition that we often fell partly through them. In some cases we had to build causeways with the assistance of the local natives, whom we paid with empty petrol tins, and it was often uncertain whether we should get across before the causeway was swept away, the water banking up behind it.

*A risky ferry river crossing*

We found the population a very happy one, and we never made a halt without receiving presents of fruit, milk, etc.

Minna was a centre for the influx of a great number of gold prospectors, mostly Syrians and Greeks, and strangers were closely watched by the police. We had one rather amusing experience; driving round the town, we found that our long car was being dogged by an Austen Seven. Eventually it caught us up and a very tall policeman unfolded himself, came over, and wished us good-day, and then asked me, "Where are you from?"

"Kano."

"Pretty country there; mining?"

"No, going to Lagos."

"Where are you from?"

"Kano!"

Suspiciously; "Kano?"

"Well, Kano, Stanleyville, Nairobi, Livingstone, Johannesburg, Cape Town."

Leaning very close; "Where did you say?"

Self, now annoyed; "Australia, New Zealand, Tasmania, Java, Ceylon, India, Burma, Ass----"

"I'm sorry, I'm most frightfully deaf. Will you come up to my house? My wife will be glad to see you."

We then visited his house, where his wife interpreted, and, more to the point, marvellous woman, fed us on a succession of plates of bacon, sausages and eggs, a meal the like of which we hadn't had for months.

The road now improved considerably, and we travelled at quite a decent speed, so that when, turning a corner, a fully grown leopard leapt in front of the car, our worn brakes failed to pull us up in time to avoid running right over it. It must have passed between the front wheels and been turned on its back by the axle, for its claws tore away part of our battery box and made large scratches on the floor boards, but it couldn't have been badly hurt because it came out from underneath, took a terrific bound into the bush, and disappeared.

Our next stop was Bida, a town which used once to be a centre for native glass manufacture. Now most of the glassware consists of old bottles.

We crossed the River Niger by means of the railway bridge, which rests on two spans running from the banks to Jebba Island in the middle, and could plainly see the famous Ju-Ju rock in midstream, where black hens, goats and cattle, and probably the odd human being, are still sacrificed to the Ju-Ju.

*The famous Ju-Ju rock*

Ibadin, Iflorin and Abeokuta, the native educational centre, were the largest native towns we had seen in Africa. They were hideous places,

129

mostly built of corrugated iron. We were now back on a tarred road, running through endless cocoa plantations and among terrific mahogany, cottonwood and banana trees to Lagos. I had never seen cocoa trees before and could not at first make out why they were being cultivated. It must be one of the few plants that have the fruit and seed growing directly on the trunk and main branches. The fruit looks like badly made bright yellow toy Rugger [rugby] balls.

*[Cocoa pods]*

We found Lagos very hard to compare with any other town. It straggles along the water front, the lagoon from which it gets its name lying behind, and is populated mainly by natives, from the type who imitate the clothes and manners of the European, down to the almost nude natives coming in from the interior with produce to sell. It is perhaps more like one of the big Indian towns than anything else.

We soon made a number of friends and spent some pleasant days at Tarkwa Bay, sailing on the lagoon, and visiting the Ikoyi Club in the evening. We were stopping with a representative of the Shell Company in a house that outdid the natives for decoration, being painted in bright yellow, red and blue. A story had it that one of the Shell employees, being under notice, had taken his revenge on the last job given him and had it painted like that.

A visit to the Residency, where the Resident was making preparations to leave to take up the Governorship of Honduras, produced the usual information that we could not continue, owing to the road, if any, being closed, but we were too used to this to let it worry us.

Before leaving Lagos we were the guests of honour of the Oba at his Iga, and here is a Press cutting giving an account of our visit; a very good example of the local journalistic style:-

*"THE OSE AT IGA IDUNGANRAND*

*"On Saturday last the 2nd of June, 1934, Falolu, the Oba of the House of Docemo held a big Ose in the Iga Opo Ide in Iga Idungganran according to ancient custom at 4 o'clock in the afternoon."*

*"There were present:- The Oba, Chief Eletu Odibo, Chief Olumegbon, Chief Oluwa, Chief Oloto, Chief Omtolo, War Chiefs Ashogbon and Oshodi, the Omo Obas, the Ibigas, and the Ilu Committee."*

*"At 5 o'clock, the Oba received the Two British Travellers, Mr. A. E. Filby and Mr. Applin, who were accompanied by Mr. W. Wells Palmer, the famous and popular Barrister who represented the late Prince Eshugbayi Eleko and the House of Docemo three years ago in the Courts of Nigeria and in the Privy Council in London in conclusion of the ten years struggle for the rights and liberty of that much-injured subject of His Majesty the King."*

*"They were received in the Iga Opo Ide with a great ovation. Mr. Wells Palmer in an interesting speech (interpreted to the Oba by Mr. Herbert Macaulay, C. E., Minister Plenipotentiary of the House of Docemo), greeted Falolu the Oba, recapitulated briefly the successful legal battles of this ancient house, and congratulated the Oba, before introducing the travellers, who walked up to the Dias and shook hands with the Oba of the House of Docemo."*

*"The Oba then instructed the Chief Oluwa to reply and greet the two travellers welcome to Nigeria. Mr. Filby acknowledged the courtesy of the Oba, who afterwards ordered Kola nuts to be distributed in native fashion to the visitors, who withdrew at half-past 5 o'clock."*

*"Mr. Filby and Mr. Applin left England on the 4th of March 1931 [incorrect] and started their long trip to Africa. They crossed the Continent of Europe under terrific snowstorms after which they struck the delightful climate of Alexandria to their great relief and pleasure. From there they proceded on a short journey to that most interesting of all towns, Cairo, the busy capital of modern Egypt on the right bank of the River Nile, the longest river in Africa. They visited the three great Pyramids of Egypt near Cairo on the left bank of the Nile, the largest of which was built 8,650 years before Christ and measures 764 feet square at its base and 480 feet in height. While visiting other places of interest here, they met Herr Horst Milleaur who was also proceding to South Africa and who presently*

*paid a visit to Lagos. They journeyed to Luxor, a village adjoining Karnack in Upper Egypt near the site of ancient Thebes the ruined ancient capital, in the Valley of which important archeological discoveries of the Kings of Egypt were made in the year 1623. They had their first taste of Desert conditions soon after they left Luxor until they reached Wadi Halfa the frontier town of the Soudan where the road had completely disappeared."*

*"This necessitated their striking out into the wastes of the desert, travelling almost entirely by compass; but fortunately they experienced no serious trouble, save the nerve-racking experience of being caught in a Mabboub or Sandstorm."*

*"In passing through the Sudd areas of the lower Sudan they had great difficulty; but the fine main roads of Uganda were a pleasing contrast which gave pleasure and relief. The wonderful animal life of Kenya Colony and Protectorate (British East Africa) with its 17,285 Europeans and 56,903 Non-Europeans exclusive of Africans was very interesting and attractive as they passed through the mandated territory of Tanganyika southwards to Northern and Southern Rhodesia the Transvaal Orange Free State and Cape Province."*

*"The original plan of the two travellers was to return to England by Sea from Cape Town, but it occurred to them that they had not seen half of the great and wonderful sights of Africa at the end of that trip; so they soon mapped a fresh route that will take them around the attractive territory of the Cape, at the same time taking in all the main towns along the coast line up to Lorenzo Marques the port and capital of Portuguese East Africa on Delagoa Bay. From here they travelled inland to the age-old Zimbabwe ruins; and went across to Bulawayo where they visited, on the Motopo Hills, that most impressive of all memorials, the last resting place of the Rt. Hon. Cecil John Rhodes, the British patriot to whom England owes the extension of her Empire from the Transvaal to the Zambesi and far beyond it to Lake Tanganyika over a vast region now called in his honour Rhodesia. Leaving there, the travellers halted a few days at the Victoria Falls on the Zambesi River at a point 900 miles from the Sea, which are admitted to be as great and noble as the Niagra Falls; but in the opinion of the two travellers, the Victoria Falls far surpass the Niagra Falls in impressiveness, being over a mile and a quarter at the lip with over 400 feet fall, while the spray from the falls can be seen four-and-forty miles away, which is responsible the native name "the smoke that thunders".*

*"Nyasaland and most of the big lakes in the great rift valley were visited. It is extremely hard to realise, they declare, that these vast areas of water are all fresh."*

*"They both made hunting trips into the Serengeti Plains and the Ngorogoro Crater where Mr. Applin was able to secure some really excellent trophies of lion, elephant, rhinoceros, etc. From here they took the course to Buti Oba on Lake Albert, where, for the first time, their Car was put on board of a vessel for the 2½ hours crossing into the Belgian Congo, where probably the most interesting experience was the week the two of them spent in the huge Ituri forest visiting tribes of Pigmies, etc."*

*"The remainder of the route to Lagos was through French Equatorial Africa, the mandated territory of the Cameroons into Nigeria at Maidugari, the Provincial Headquarters of the Bornu Province southwest of Lake Tchad."*

*"Up to the present, the journey has covered about three-and-twenty thousand miles of three in length, throughout which Mr. Filby cannot think of any stretch which had not provided some real point of interest; while he finds it extremely interesting to compare one part of Africa with another. To the two travellers, one thing has impressed them very forcibly as being the same throughout the whole Continent; and that is, the delightful hospitality of the people whom they have had the pleasure of meeting everywhere."*

However, it was a most interesting experience. Pandemonium broke loose on our arrival at the Iga; fifty drums, cymbals, brass bells and horns crashed out their welcome, while the Oba's subjects pressed round us and shouted greetings, and were only prevented from following us into the audience chamber by the stalwart guards.

The Oba was a handsome lean-jawed man, looking extraordinarily young for his sixty years. He was wearing a white silk hat shaped rather like a mitre and a beautiful white silk robe. On a chair next to him stood a gilt crown about two feet in height, also a large gilt tortoise. To his right sat the princes of the blood and to the left the nobles took their ease. Behind them sat the white-capped chiefs under the leadership of a splendid-looking man who was introduced to us as the War Lord. Those who were presented, prostrated themselves at full length on the floor in front of the Oba, and speech was conducted through an interpreter, as it was not considered courteous to address the Oba direct.

Our interpreter's account of our travels was received with prolonged applause, and we then proffered our present of two bottles of gin, the traditional gift of the early traders, and received in exchange two of the royal four-sectioned Kola nuts. These nuts are highly valued by the natives for their sustaining powers. Normally they grow with three sections or divisions, and it is one of the royal prerogatives that any Kola nut with four sections is the property of the chief. Before handing the nuts to us the Prime Minister took a large bite of each, and we afterwards learnt that this was to prove the nuts were not poisoned. A convenient method of poisoning is to insert a piece of metal in a Kola nut and let it remain for some hours, when the juice of the nut in contact with the metal forms a powerful poison.

A curious custom of the royal house is that the Oba's bed is set above the grave of his fathers, which is twenty feet deep, and when he dies he will also be buried there and the bed of his successor will occupy the same place.

The rank of Oba does not descend to the children of the Oba but to the princes of the blood royal.

When we took our leave, our departure was accompanied by a peculiar clicking noise, produced by the entire company snapping three fingers of one hand against the palm of the other.

It was almost necessary to fight our way out through the crowds swarming round the doors. A loud chant started up and a very aged woman began to lead a dance, then rushing forward took my hand and, speaking to the crowd, who answered with a roar of applause ending in a long-drawn "Aaaaah!" she pointed to my hair, the extreme fairness of which seems to intrigue all the natives I have met.

Our interpreter had been a Mr. Macaulay, the editor of one of the local papers, and a descendant of the famous Black Bishop.

*[Samuel Adjai Crowther, The "Black Bishop"]*

134

[Samuel Adjai Crowther was the first bishop of Niger and the first Anglican bishop. He had been a slave, but became an explorer, translator and staunch abolitionist.]

A visit to Macaulay's house was full of interest. He had many stories to tell of the old slave days, while his collection of curios included the royal baton and dancing sword and the old seal of the kings of Lagos.

The following day was King George V's birthday, and at eight a. m. we were out on the racecourse watching the parade, the native regiment giving a striking display of efficiency and smartness in their uniform of shorts, putties, shirts with bright red seams contrasting with yellow facings, and small *tarbooshes* [small feathered headwear]. The Governor took the salute amid a colourful scene gay with the native princes in their bright clothes shaded by gaudy umbrellas, from whose crowded ranks came a long-drawn sigh as each of the twenty rounds of the salute were fired from a light battery.

Just before we left, Lagos was struck by a terrific typhoon, the rain being so heavy that visibility was little more than ten feet, and I afterwards learnt that three inches of rain had fallen in under an hour. Our departure in the morning was delayed by Applin going down with a bad bout of malaria, but in the evening he felt much better and we went out to the Ikoyi Club where I had a great time in the swimming bath.

# Chapter 18 ~ Nigeria ~ Benin ~ Togo ~ Ghana

The next day, Applin was so much better that we started, being given a send-off by the many friends we had made. The first part of the road was back through cocoa plantations through which we had come. We then started bearing westward, passing through Papalanto and into the heavily wooded area near Ilaro and Ado, where we again passed through large cocoa plantations. The road, being built merely to serve these, was getting rougher and rougher as we progressed.

About three in the afternoon, the track in front of us was, we noticed, coloured a brilliant green, and we decided to investigate before continuing. It was well for us that we did, for the green proved to be a curious floating weed, something between a lily and grass, covering the surface of one of the lagoons that form a chain along the Gulf of Guinea. High walls of papyrus had shut out the lagoon itself and we could quite easily have mistaken it for a continuation of our road. There was, however, a pontoon, and although the road was closed owing to the rains and therefore the pontoon was officially out of commission, we managed to persuade the native guardians to take us over.

We crossed the lagoon, which was the colour of strong tea, and entered the mangroves on the other bank.

Many of the villages were actually built in the shallow waters of these lagoons, the houses being set on stilts and surrounded by long lines of fencing, which formed fish-traps along which the natives patrolled in their dugouts.

On the borders of Dahomey [Benin] we were held up at the Douane's [Customs] office, but I persuaded them to send us into the main town of Porto Novo with a police escort so that we could explain our case direct to the authorities. Our escort had a wild ride sitting on the water tanks on the running-board, and twice we had to stop to pick up a dropped rifle. The French immigration and Customs authorities were not satisfied with my story, and said we could not stop in the country, so I agreed to leave immediately, but left via Grand Popo and the other border, so that we crossed the country without trouble.

Our route, which was through endless coconut groves that came right down to the shore, was plentifully decorated with the small fetish houses of the natives, usually little mud-built thatched shrines housing crude earth figures before which were set offerings of food.

*The Grand Popo, Dahomey - A Portuguese church*

We had to cross several more lagoons and Congo, our monkey, caused great excitement each time by attacking the native paddlers, as he now acted as an excellent guardian and would not let anyone except ourselves approach the car.

The scenery along the coast can best be described as palms, palms, and then more palms. From our camps we were able to watch the bumboats [small boats] unloading cargo from ships anchored outside the terrific swell of the waves. The boats would ride in on the surf, with the boys paddling frantically, and twice we saw these experts upset with all their cargo, most of which appeared to float and was afterwards towed ashore by boys who swam alongside of each piece. It was an interesting proceeding to watch the helmsman, perched on the stern, steering with a long oar. He could watch the waves rolling in, and when he saw what he judged to be a good opportunity, his shouts would produce redoubled efforts by the paddlers, and then, when the boat was poised on the crest of the wave, some twenty feet in the air and fifty feet from the shore, the boys would throw their paddles overboard and follow them into the surf, not diving but just tumbling in, so that here a leg and there a head showed for a moment before they were all swallowed in the trough of the wave. The boat, with only the helmsman on board, would then surge onto the beach, where it was hauled up by a waiting party, leaving the crew to swim ashore.

Entering Togoland [Togo], the country became more hilly. We passed through Lomi and Palomi, where we spent a hectic evening with the representatives of the United Africa Company. The delicious fruits of the wild paw-paw grew in profusion along our route and supplied a welcome addition to our meals.

At one native village, we ran into a festival where women carried long poles with bunches of ribbons attached to the top, while the younger ones wore hats made of straw in the shape of toppers [top hats]. The men wore hideous masks and carried long swords and ancient rifles studded with brass tacks and bound with copper wire. All of them were plentifully covered with red mud, for they had been dancing all night. The leaders, however, were nattily attired in suits of European cut, but made of pink floral satin or red cotton, and they invariably carried umbrellas. I afterwards discovered that this was the Society of the Lost Lamb! No comments! [I have no idea what my uncle means by this.]

If you ask one of the natives what nationality he is, he will invariably reply "French" instead of giving his native tribe. This country was, of course, formerly German, and during their occupation they taught the natives to speak pidgin English so that they should not understand their masters' private conversations, so they are former German subjects, speaking English, and governed by the French through Geneva.

The day's run was a long one, and night had already fallen when we entered Accra, where we had decided to enjoy the luxury of a hotel, but the trouble was to find one. Driving along the tarred roads, we saw a typical Englishman, stick in hand, taking his evening walk, and we stopped to enquire the way. He proved to be Sergeant McCabe of the Royal West African Frontier Forces and his suggestion that he could describe the way better if he explained it over a beer at his house resulted in our being his guests for nearly two weeks. During that time we got to know Accra well, shooting at the range, visiting the Club, and wandering about the colourful streets. We were also picking up the curious pidgin English, finding some difficulty in understanding such things as "Lef' small" meaning soon, and "Footie done bloke", meaning a punctured tyre, and other strange phrases.

We also paid a visit to the Rodger Club at their grand Homowo Dance, and were much amused by the contrast between those who, dressed in correct evening dress, danced modern European dances in perfect style, and those who, in their own normal dress, danced something closely resembling the Big Apple, the floor being kept from overcrowding by the police, who wandered up and down with whips and struck out impartially, which seemed to add to the fun.

A daily call was made at the Slip Inn, a bar run by the Ice Company, and on the way there I particularly liked hearing the Hausa story-tellers who sat in the street recounting stories to an appreciative audience. They always started off by saying, "A story, a story, let it come, let it go," and finished with, "Off with the rat's head".

The native women looked very attractive in their gay clothes, native chiefs wandered up and down the streets, followed by their retainers, while the native shops bore such strange legends as, "Slowly, Softly One Catches Monkey Vulcanising Works", or "Print/Develop-Ing".

One afternoon we accepted the invitation of the Governor (Northcote) who was much interested in our travels, to visit Christianborg Castle, situated on a rocky promontory overlooking the Bight of Benin.

*Christianborg Castle, near Freetown, Sierra Leone*

The old gateway bears the date 1790 and the castle was built in the days of Christian VI of Denmark, and has passed through the hands of the Danes, the Portuguese and the English, as well as having been held by the natives under Asameni, who I understand took it from the Portuguese by a trick. The natives came to buy rifles at the castle, but had to leave their arms outside. They made the request that they should be allowed to test their purchases by firing one shot out to sea. Having loaded, they turned on the occupants and captured the castle.

The battery in the courtyard, through the paving of which grew a large tree, bore the date 1734, while as we went down to the old slave-dungeons we saw many of the ancient rifles preserved on the walls.

McCabe was leaving on a tour of inspection, and we decided to go with him and had a wonderful run along the coast. Near Cape Coast the shores were littered with guns; French guns, Swedish guns, English guns, but all old guns, while the fort was in a remarkable state of preservation. We entered through the old dungeons built to hold thousands of slaves. Long ago the fort and its trade were a valuable source of revenue to the English Crown. The dungeons themselves are cut out of the solid rock and have a wonderful domed roof. In one part a brick facing had been put on the wall to cover up a famous Ju-Ju rock, and it was very easy, standing there in the semi-gloom, to imagine the thousands of manacled slaves praying to their gods.

The remains of old shackles still littered the floors, while iron cannon balls and grapeshot filled the powder store, where there was a very ornate brick staircase. It seemed curious that this should have been built here in the dark underground, as it is obvious that the naked lights of those days could not have been carried into this store and therefore the elaborate ornamentation was entirely wasted.

Climbing onto the bastion we inspected the battery of twenty-pounders that commanded the sea wall, pyramids of ball still piled at their base as if ready for action.

Below were further batteries, and below again were guns that had been tumbled from the walls to the beach.

Dr. Dyce Sharp, who kindly conducted us round, was an authority on the history of the coastal forts. He had in his possession a twenty-four-pounder and had traced an authentic record of its having fired a ball one thousand one hundred yards. This is of particular interest, as I believe it is the only known record giving the range of these guns.

A visit was also paid to the old fortified lighthouse. This, too, was bristling with guns, a specially interesting one being a huge fellow with two *fleur-de-lys* in the barrel with a large "P" superimposed, and we speculated whether it had originally been captured from the French by the pirates who infested this coast.

Dr. Dyce Sharp told us it was almost certain that Columbus had visited this coast and that it is more than possible he contemplated starting his famous voyage from here, and it is curious to think that history was in the making here long before America was discovered.

We also visited the perfectly preserved fort of Elmina further along the coast with its large double moat and drawbridge, before continuing to the new port of Takoradi.

While there, we went to Allen's Hotel, a great centre for the prospectors after their trips up country. As it was midday, the usual gin-party was in session, in fact in full swing, and we found that the native barman was inadvertently serving water with a dash of Angostura, to which the drinkers were blissfully adding more water to weaken it.

While we were there, a chap in a high state of nervousness asked us if we were returning to Accra that night, and when we said we were, asked us to carry an important letter back with us. As far as I could gather, he was the director of the local prison, and he had to hang a man in two days' time. Although an appeal had gone through, it had been wrongly dated, and he would have to hang this man unless it was presented in Accra within a certain time. He was vastly relieved when we agreed to take it, and told us that he hated these hangings, as they were not exactly profitable. He received two pounds, out of which he gave one pound to the sergeant in charge, two and six to each assistant, and then the doctor and witness came to his house and drank twenty-five shillings worth of drink.

The return to Accra was accomplished without incident, and we continued our round of sundowner parties and palm-oil chop and ground-nut stew parties, which are big features in the Coast entertaining. Apart from these two interesting dishes, these parties started off with a terrific beer-drink. At the last one I went to, barrels of beer were provided and each guest was given a tankard and told that the barrels had to be emptied before the meal began. Starting at noon we sat down to eat at four p.m.

"Gold" was the word that was passing round the clubs and bars as Europeans arrived from the interior, while diamonds were being mined some hundred miles inland, and we began to feel the urge of the gold fever.

We were still staying with McCabe, who proved himself a charming host with a comprehensive knowledge of Irish politics, and listening to his soothing brogue I got quite a new insight into the affairs of that country. However, our circle was soon to be broken up; McCabe had orders to join his regiment at Kumasi, and the same day Applin decided to join a gold prospector in the northern territories.

I was sorry to see him go, as he had been a great partner and we had enjoyed a good safari together. I had another slight touch of malaria, and visited the hill station of Aburi, a wonderful spot a thousand feet above sea level and reserved as an experimental ground for the planting of trees and plants from every part of the world.

Immediately opposite the resthouse was a tall cottonwood tree with a large buttress-shaped base and a straight trunk studded with knobbles and spikes. One of the guests there told me it towered a hundred and fifty-nine feet into the air, and I think he must have had a passion for calculating heights, for the next time I met him, about two years later, he was staring at the top of St. Paul's Cathedral.

After a few days' rest, I felt much better and returned to Accra, to find everyone in a very cheerful frame of mind, as a levy on salaries had been removed. But I couldn't see that they were much better off, as the price of whisky had gone up.

People were very wroth with the armchair politicians at home, as it seemed that the natives had been agitating for the Governor's removal, and while he was on leave he had deservedly been promoted to a higher position and would not return, and the general opinion among the natives was that he had been removed as a result of their agitation, whereas if he had come back for a short period it would have made things much easier for his successor.

# Chapter 19 ~ Ghana

I decided to carry on with only Congo the monkey for company, and as usual I was told that there was no direct road to Kumasi. Congo, however, assured me that he knew the way. I went down to the port, intending to take some fresh fish with me, but found I could not get any, as I had struck the day when the fishing fleet, though it put to sea as usual, did not attempt to catch fish, this being one of the rites of the fishermen's particular Ju-Ju.

Pushing into heavily-wooded country, my first stop was with the District Commissioner at Kribbi, and my arrival coincided with that of several other travellers, so we had a hectic evening and played greyhound racing until three a.m.

I found that there had once been a road through this way, which had been allowed to fall into disuse, as there was another one further to the west. I had great difficulty in crossing small rivers on the two main supporting tree trunks which was all that was left of the bridges. It was ticklish work balancing on these, and Congo's antics on my head did not improve matters.

Vegetation had grown so quickly that I was passing through a tunnel of greenery which was fast being filled with creepers that dragged across the roof of the car. It was here I came across a group of excited natives who told me that one of their number had just been crushed by a large snake.

I left Congo in charge of the car and climbed a weather-beaten mountain track to the high plateau which is said to be the place where the Ashanti fled during the conquest of the country. On top I found excellent roads carrying a fair amount of motor traffic. There was now a road up the mountain, but originally cars had been carried up in parts by native bearers and reassembled at the top.

The Bassel Mission, one of the oldest in the country, had a store there and from it I could see the square-cut face of the Ju-Ju rock Bukirous.

One of the Kevatu natives told me that the missionaries make "plenty trouble" with their ideas of "one man, one wife" as there was now a great surplus of women and their price had gone down to four shillings each.

Although I had great difficulty in forcing a passage between the large tree-trunks, as the exposed roots tipped the car at all angles, I got to Kumasi and defeated the experts who had told me it was impossible.

I called on McCabe, who gave me an invitation to the N. C. O.'s [Non-Commissioned Officer's] mess, where I heard a singsong by one of the finest groups of men I have ever met. "Singing Cockles, Alive Alive-o" was rendered in parade-ground voices that I thought would bring the mess down.

During the evening, Congo had gone on an exploration trip of his own and I had a telephone call from the Ridge, where the officers had their quarters, to say that my partner had introduced himself to most of them and was regaling himself on presents of bananas.

From here to Tamali the road was good, but there the District Commissioner told me that I could go very little further owing to the rains. However, I carried on.

At one camp, Congo succumbed to the blandishments of a lady friend. He kept coming back to the top of a tree and looking down at me as much as to say, "I hate to leave you, old boy, but these women are the devil," so I had to wish him luck and wondered if he would produce a new species of monkey in this part of the world which was so many miles from his home.

I missed his comforting weight on my shoulder and his cheeping comments as we drove. He would have liked the two hundred horsemen I met prancing along to the sound of drums and cymbals and carrying ancient Dane guns.

The District Commissioner caught me up in his car and told me I was in trouble for not paying fares on the many ferries I had crossed. The natives in charge had presented me with a book which I had signed, not realising that they thought I was in the political service, as only District Commissioners and Governors were allowed to fly the Union Jack on their cars as I did. Matters were squared up, and I continued, but was eventually stopped by the White Volta River, which was in flood.

It was obvious that I could not cross, and I decided that as my late partner, Applin, was prospecting in the district, I would leave the car and join him. A small village chief offered to look after the car, and had a thatch of leaves built over it. He also offered guides and porters to find my friend.

Before leaving, I walked down to the river to see if there was any possible means of getting the car across, but could see none. Turning to retrace my steps, I found two fully-grown lions observing my movements with flattering interest. If I did not want to act as the main course for their breakfast, it seemed the only way out was to jump into the flooded river, which was almost as bad. I waved my arms and said "Shoo!" which so disconcerted them that - one wrinkling his nose in a silent snarl - they turned and walked off in disgust.

A long line of porters, carrying my kit on their heads, filed after me down to the river, and we crossed in crazy dugouts, then struck off into the sparse forest.

During our frequent rests, my porters collected a number of green skinned fruit a little bigger than a walnut, with a large kernel, which made pleasant eating. I afterwards learnt that they were known as Shea-butter, which is used extensively in the manufacture of women's lipsticks, so I may have tasted them again since then.

*Crossing the river on dugouts*

My guide took me directly to where Applin was camped without any hesitation, and I then joined him in his prospecting. Every day we followed outcrops of rock, the natives breaking off pieces all along the line, which were put into bags, labelled, and brought to camp in the evening to be crushed with pestle and mortar and washed to see if they contained gold.

From our last camp, we made a twelve-mile trek over rocky hills and through swamps, followed by our string of porters, to a village called Zanlaregn, where we were told an interesting story of how, twenty years before, two white prospectors had entered an area renowned for Ju-Ju and had discovered a very valuable gold deposit, but had to flee from the enraged natives, who overtook them, killing one and badly wounding the other, who died later babbling of fabulous gold reefs.

We decided to investigate. The witch doctor was sounded and after suitable presents had been given, including two black chickens which were to be sacrificed to the Ju-Ju, we were told we could investigate in two days' time.

Our boys and the porters were terrified at the idea, some of them deserting immediately, while our head boy informed us that a spell had been put on us and this spell, among other things, would prevent us from shooting any more game in the forest.

From our camp we could see one of the large bush turkeys that are plentiful in most parts of Africa, feeding on a small flat clearing below us, and we made up our minds that here was the very opportunity to disprove the spell theory and to acquire a welcome addition to our larder.

Our gun bearers would not accompany us, but took up observation posts with the remainder of the boys to watch operations.

Applin was carrying a shotgun and I a .22 rifle. I think I can claim to be a reasonably good shot and there is no doubt that Applin was an expert. We took great care in stalking our game and got within twenty yards of the turkey. I then took unhurried aim and fired - with no result whatever. We looked at each other in surprise, as the bird continued placidly feeding, then Applin let drive with both barrels of his shotgun, whereupon the bird took wing and landed only a little way off. Four times we stalked the bird and fired from close range before it flew away and we had to return to an empty camp.

Threatening thunder clouds darkened the sky as the witch doctor, in ceremonial dress, with a necklace of teeth and a girdle of bones, conducted us to the Ju-Ju ground, which proved to be a very disappointing clearing among some rocks where two doll-like figures made of earth looked pop-eyed at us as we searched.

We soon came across the prospector's discovery, for a vein over two inches wide showed an almost dull red-gold, and I thought our fortunes were made, but Applin's verdict was that it was only pyrites, locally known as Readite, and absolutely valueless.

*Tanganyika border. This gold mine is worked solely by one man.*

Applin now decided to return to his headquarters at Nangodi and I accompanied him, but found that I was far from welcome with his employers. The District Commissioner had mentioned to them my delinquency in not having paid the ferry dues, and as they were on an amazing gold find they did not want trouble with the authorities and my presence was considered most undesirable.

Their excuse was that the rains were approaching, and they had only enough whisky for those already there before communications were cut off and they were unable to obtain more.

So I trekked towards the French border for a short distance and made camp in a wonderfully decorated resthouse.

Applin joined me in the evening, bringing a very welcome bottle of the precious whisky, but went back soon after nightfall, leaving me with a guttering candle stuck in an empty bottle as my only company.

I suppose the Ju-Ju palaver had made me nervous, for I was very loath to get under the mosquito netting and blow out the candle, situated as I was on my own, miles from another white man in a country where I could not understand one word of the naked savages.

Frogs kept up an unholy chant in the swamps, while the monotonous call of the fever-bird came from the branches of a ghostly baobab tree that I could just see outside. First the bird would give a series of three notes, repeated with maddening regularity, and then, when I got used to counting three, it would stop at two, leaving me waiting for the third, and when I had got used to two it would change to one or back to three.

Inside, the mosquitoes were arriving in swarms, setting up a shrill vibrant noise like the hum of a pygmy dynamo; then an enormous bat flew into the wall and dropped to the floor, scrabbling along and then flying out of the black hole of the door again.

I must have dropped off to sleep, for at about midnight, I was awakened by a terrific crash of thunder. Sitting up in bed I could see by the light of the candle, three tall nude ghost-like figures that bowed and knelt and rose again, water dripping from their glistening bodies.

The weird mouthing noises they made convinced me that they were human, and I guessed they were natives who had come in to shelter from the downpour of the storm. Glad of any company in that eerie spot, I made signs that they could sleep on the floor, but they sat bunched together like three lost spooks, and when I woke I found them in the same position, still staring at me.

In the morning, Applin arrived with a string of porters, and I did a seventeen mile trek to the Black Volta River and then another to the car, which I rescued from its thatching and started back to the coast again, having a very difficult run, and having to live on native food nearly the whole way. I missed bread very much but drank gallons of tea, of which I had plenty.

It would obviously be some time before I could expect the roads to be fit to travel on again, and I had been very lucky to get back, for several vehicles heavier than mine had bogged down and would be unable to move for months, and I decided to get a job in one of the mines up country.

The United Africa Company, who seem to have an interest in everything that goes on in West Africa, kindly offered to store my car free, and I went up country to a mine that is now famous, but in those days had only just been prospected - Marlu.

*Elmina Castle*

En route, as if I had not had enough of ghosts, I spent a lonely night in the haunted castle of Elmina. The drawbridge was raised and I was left alone on the moonlit bastion, listening to the waves hitting the front of the fort with a deep booming noise which echoed down into the dungeons below, but I rather enjoyed it.

# Chapter 20 ~ Ghana

A train took me up as far as Insu and from there a mine lorry took me over the newly constructed road to the mine itself. Here, on the strength of my one underground visit in Jo'burg, I applied for a job as a miner. I was advised to go a mile or so further on and see a contractor who was very short of men, and I wandered along a track that was being marked out for a road and up to a roughly-built shack from which issued the most gorgeous stream of profanity I have ever heard. As boldly as possible I walked in and stated that I wanted a job, to be met with:-

"What the hell do you know about mining?"

"Nothing," said I.

"Fine, you've got the job; you're the first bloke that's been honest. D'you know anything about paying out?"

"Yes," said I.

"Fine. There's two thousand boys; pay 'em."

With that I was left with a mass of grubby-looking pencilled notes and a safe full of money, and with the assistance of several native clerks I got down to the job. At the end of the day I found I was eighteen pounds on the wrong side, and thought it would be the shortest job I had ever held. Hearing a flow of profanity approaching, I got ready to set out on my travels again, but having reported the deficit, I was surprised to hear that it was "bloody good" and the nearest they had got to being correct since he had been on the job.

That night camp beds were set up in the pay office, and over a bottle I discovered he was an Australian, and as I knew Australia well, we soon became good friends. And then I found he was the individual who had come to our rescue near El Shellal on our downward trip.

During the evening, he told me he had been working at high pressure for several months, and he could not leave the job, as there was no-one who could be left in charge, the only other white men being Italians, who, although excellent workers, could not control the natives. He had been suffering from violent toothache, and proposed that I should take charge while he went to Kumasi to have the tooth extracted, so that night I became a fully-fledged mine manager, or at least I had been put in charge of tunnels burrowing themselves into the sides of a hill and a lot of holes in the ground.

My employer did not intend leaving for a while, and told me that while he was there, I was to learn as much as possible about the work, but not give away the fact that I knew so little. On the first day one of the Italians took me on a tour of inspection, but as he didn't speak much English and I very little Italian, I didn't learn much. I did gather, however, that we were not actually mining, but proving an area, which meant that prospecting tunnels were being driven through the hill and at frequent intervals, geologists and surveyors would descend on us to examine our progress. I always went in with them, and they gave me some valuable tips, but their advice was far too technical, as they did not realise that I knew nothing at all about the job.

However, I worked on a system of trial and error. For instance, I noticed they all carried sticks with a small iron pick-head attached, and as soon as they got underground, they would poke the roof and mutter that it would have to come off or that it was O.K. I had a pick made for me to my own design by the native blacksmith, and going underground with my lamp-bearers, interpreters and head men, I took what I thought was a professional poke at the roof, and only just missed the ton or so of rock that came crashing down. My staff looked at me to see what would happen next, so I yelled at them to find out who the hell was responsible, to fine him part of his pay, and get things right at once, although I had no idea what "right" was. Anyway, it worked wonderfully, and my stock went up considerably. I later discovered that the professional pokers of roofs could tell by the sound made by their pickheads on the roof whether it was loose or not.

I found that the tunnels were called "adits" and the smaller ones off them were known as "crosscuts". Numbers of these adits ran in from the hillside at three different levels, some of them going in to a distance of six hundred feet, and from these, crosscuts were driven to join each other.

Our workings were constantly joining up with old native workings which had long fallen into disuse, and were now the home of thousands of bats, and when we accidentally broke through into one of these, the bats would come streaming out, putting out the lights and smelling vilely as they flapped into my face and got up my shorts. I was always on the lookout for ancient tools, as it was more than possible that these were the famous King Solomon's Mines.

Gradually I had more and more to do. Gangs had to be directed in the felling of heavy timber to make room for the power houses; others worked on the cutting of new roads, and others shifted light railway lines to form new dumps. Besides all this, I had to make a twice-daily visit to the fifty faces that were being worked. A "face" is the end of a tunnel that is being hewn out.

I had observed that a few yards behind the working party, two pieces of string with stones attached were nailed to the roof, and on my first visit with my employer, I had seen him get behind these and then tell the head boy to move a lamp up and down on the face. Without the slightest idea what this procedure meant, I religiously copied it, with the result that the tunnels began to assume the most marvellous curves. My plotting of the underground workings was the only one in our possession, and it soon became obvious that crosscuts being tunnelled from opposite directions should have met days before, so I had a great game going to one end and telling workers in the other crosscut, which should have met ours, to bang on the wall. I would then listen at my end, and if I could hear anything, direct operations, up, down or sideways, according to the direction of the sound, causing most caustic comments when my employer eventually visited the spot and, turning a sharp corner in what should have been a straight and level tunnel, abruptly fall down a hole. He explained, in picturesque language, that the use of the string device was to keep the tunnels straight.

I never quite gathered what our contract was, but I understood that he was paid for every foot of ground that was taken out. Day after day new gangs of natives were employed; usually they would work under dignified Hausa subcontractors, but they all had to be watched carefully, and the cry was always "more footage". Daylight or dark the work went ahead, and my employer kept a vast ice-chest of drinks for when we began to feel the strain, and a bottle of champagne was always available.

The tents of the forerunners of the construction engineers gradually got closer to us, and our hut became a meeting place for visitors in the evenings and at weekends.

The talk ran on shop and jumped from accounts of mining in Egypt to Brazil, Rio Grande, Venezuela, and everywhere the bright metal had been found. A lone prospector, far ahead of our camp, paid us periodical visits. He was a great old chap, known to all as Brum, and I soon became one of his favourites. In the course of his career he had been a music-hall artist, and then had gone in for mining. He had been in the Klondyke rush and many others, and was of the opinion that the rush at Kalgoorlie, in Australia, had been far the toughest. His stories ranged from Kalgoorlie to Coolgardie; famous names such as Bendigo Jane and Carrie, were frequently mentioned. Then another member of the party would interrupt with an eye-witness account of the finding of the Londonderry, the richest gold pocket ever known. Then would come another reminiscence from my boss of eating sausages in the Black Ranges round Lenora and Bones Creek with Franklin Roosevelt.

The conversation was sometimes difficult to follow, as it ranged with dizzying rapidity from Lake Atlin in the Yukon back to Australia and the Golden Pig and Southern Cross and the terrible shortage of water there. Someone recounts how Van Nieman was hanged for killing somebody whose name I do not catch, with a shovel; then the talk switches over to diamonds and back again to the ancient Egyptian gold mines. By this time Brum has become mellowed to a certain point, and we all know what is going to happen; he rises from his seat on a box and with a preliminary cough says he will give us a song. A high quavering note, then, "S'cuse me, folks, I gotter take my teeth out, I always swallers 'em when I gets a 'igh note". He then gives us some wonderful yodelling, which gradually fades out as he slides under the table, where he snores peacefully. The gramophone plays our one record, "Hooligan's Ball", continuously, and at a certain point one of the guests will always say, "Listen, boys" and a sly look of anticipation will appear on his face, then the record will grind out "An' down in the hall some flirtin' was heard," and conversation is resumed.

Probably the party would end, as it did one evening, by a latecomer putting his head through the door and saying, "That bloody blasting boy's blown his bloody self up again!" and we all had to go out to see what had happened.

My employer's special friend was the engineer at the main shaft that was being sunk about a mile and a half away from us. These two would vie with each other in giving elaborate dinners, and my ideas on what could be done were in great demand. Once I suggested crayfish brought direct from the coast by express train, and an order was put through, and friends who were travelling to Kumasi all promised to bring baskets up with them. We went down in one of the mine lorries to fetch the consignment from the siding, and found that a number of baskets had broken open, and the live crayfish had scuttled all over the Pullman coach, so that we delayed the train for some time while we looked under the seats for them.

These two friends had one great party trick which was always an enormous success; the Australian was well over six feet and as thin as a rake, while the engineer was very short and tubby, and when the party got sufficiently gay, they would hang the straw packing from bottles round their waists and circle round each other with beatific smiles in a hula-hula that brought down the house.

During one of these parties, the head boy arrived to say that the white surveyor in the tent nearest our camp had died, and as he belonged to the same fraternity as our hosts, they decided, with drunken gravity, that certain rites must be performed. We staggered off into the night, falling down trenches and climbing over fallen trees, until we reached the camp. A light in the tent next to that of our dead surveyor proclaimed that his partner was at home, and after much banging on the canvas, a dishevelled person appeared and asked us what the hell we wanted. With great solemnity, my two hosts explained that Brother So-and-so was lying dead in the next tent, the reply being, "To blazes with'm!" and the apparition retreated into its tent. The rite seemed to have been fulfilled, for we tramped back again and the party developed into a kind of wake.

I have perhaps conveyed that we did nothing but drink, but this was far from the truth. Never have I seen a set of men work harder or more willingly, while I have never done so much in my life. Up and shaved before daylight, I had to send off different gangs of boys, sack a few, take some others on, stop some pay from others as a punishment, doctor those that had been hurt, and perhaps provide some soap pills of my own manufacture for stomach-aches, and give judgement on any disputes that had arisen; then off to see that the light rails had been moved over to the edge of the dump to facilitate the shooting of material down the sides of the hill, then go to the stores to see that explosives had been issued before returning to a huge breakfast. Before midday I had blundered through most of the lower levels, hustling things here and altering them there; then lunch and afterwards into the levels higher up the hill and then back for a drink and a bath. It was a very welcome relief to get out of the heavy boots and mud-splashed clothing, after which I had to get the gangs ready for the night shift, see how work was progressing on the new house that was being built for us, and so add to the confusion of the native builders, as each white man who came along to look at the house had different ideas and gave instructions accordingly; and then deal with the long line of applicants who wanted jobs, most of whom brought me bribes, which I could not accept, of grain, eggs and women.

One evening, the General Manager and five others whose names are very well known in the mining world, paid us a surprise visit, and one of them, commenting on my underground work, said he had never seen anything like it, and as far as he could make out, the sole use of my tunnels was that they enabled him to go from one side of the hill to the other without getting wet. I was hurt.

My employer returned with them to Kumasi to have his tooth attended to, and I was left in charge. I soon missed the support of his forceful personality and lurid language. Quarrels broke out between the different tribes employed, in the course of which sharp shovels and sticks of explosive were used, and it was one of my most unpleasant jobs to charge into a whirling mass of shovels and yelling natives, underground and usually in the dark, and hit out indiscriminately until order was restored.

Then the pump got jammed in one of the half-constructed "winzes" (a winze is a perpendicular shaft driven from an overhead adit to one below; although at first I did not know it by this name, and when I received a letter enquiring if work was still being carried on with the winze, I thought it referred to a peculiar type of three-wheeled barrow we had, and correspondence was carried on somewhat at cross-purposes). Not knowing how to get the jammed pump out of the winze, I had a terrific job manhandling it to the surface; then when I got it going again, two boys got gassed going down too soon after blasting, so after that I hit on the ingenious idea of using one of the Italians as a miner's canary and lowering him on a rope. As long as I could hear him cursing and swearing as he looked round I knew it was O.K., but if all was silent I pulled him up again, looking rather like a pantomime demon coming up amid clouds of smoke. For this service he was rewarded with a bottle of Chianti every evening, and was well satisfied.

153

Some of my experiences underground were most unpleasant. While inspecting a face, some explosives detonated behind me, and there was a heavy fall of rock. I thought we were trapped, and had started the gang working frantically to dig us out to freedom, having a very bad spot of wind up [wind up here means being very frightened], when a party of surveyors walked up from behind who had come in from another entrance which I had forgotten, and asked what the hell all the row was about.

However, there were the lighter sides. A cheerful gang of Kroo boys, black fishermen from Sierra Leone, were working one of the top levels, but had absolutely no sense of teamwork, and I endeavoured to inculcate this by telling them, in the pidgin English of the coast, the fable of the crows who used to come and eat the farmer's corn, and as soon as he approached with a gun, would fly away to a nearby tree, so he smeared the tree with bird-lime, and the next time he approached they all flew up as usual and stuck fast, but when he came with his gun to shoot them as they stuck there, the head crow gave the word of command, "Fly!", and off they went, tearing up the tree by the roots and taking it with them. The intention of my story was of course to prove what could be done if we all worked together. I changed the crows to birds familiar to the Kroo boys and the bird-lime to sticky clay, and they all seemed to enjoy the tale greatly, so I went off rather patting myself on the back and feeling quite confident that they would all pull together much better in the future. Later in the day a frantic message was brought to me, and I went to see what had happened. Apparently all they had taken in of my story was the sticky clay, and they had smeared their tools and themselves all over with a glutinous mess and were sitting there doing nothing at all.

The geologists had a pretty tough job. They would cut out a line about six inches wide by two inches deep right along the side of the tunnel, and this material was sent back in bags, just as it was when I was prospecting with Applin, so that by this means an analysis was obtained of the whole area. One day I watched them working under particular difficulties, as we had just broken through into an old native shaft and bats were pouring past them in thousands. At the same time a long line of ants was trekking into the tunnel and incidentally up their shorts, so that they were jumping madly up and down to dislodge the ants, at the same time waving their arms to keep the bats away. At other times I would see them standing up to their waists in water in an old working that I would not have dared to enter for fear of the roof collapsing; and as they had no set working hours they were always liable to walk up to a face just when the explosives were about to be fired and the fuses already lit, and would have to beat a hasty retreat. Again, the natives would never realise that the pushing of the trucks loaded with heavy material was not a game, and would come running down the narrow tunnel with them, so that it was not unusual to see a geologist come pounding out at the end only two leaps ahead of a laden truck, but they seemed to take everything as part of the day's work.

154

My employer returned, bringing his wife with him, and the good old days were over. On the first morning after her arrival he lined the boys up as usual, and I waited for his customary flow of profanity, but, mindful of her presence, he attempted to modify his language, and stood there wildly spluttering, "You-you-you silly ass, you - you - *tram-driver*!" until he could stand it no longer, flung restraint to the winds, and continued in his normal strain.

I was getting very fed up with the work underground, which was preying on my mind to such an extent that I used to have wild nightmares of being in a tunnel and all the lamps being blown out, and would wake up yelling "Boy! Bring a light!" My employer, whose sleeping quarters were close to mine, would call out sleepily to know what was wrong, and just to save my face I would have to pretend that I had suddenly remembered something that ought to be done in the mine, and off I would have to go to have a look at it. Besides this, horizon fever was becoming strong again, so I made up my mind - next pay day would see me on my way once more.

Pay, by the way, was delivered to us at our outpost by an armed guard, and when we had signed for it, the guard would leave, and we would put it in a small safe that had been sunk in a huge block of concrete, which took six boys to lift, and I would then make my bed over it.

These precautions were not excessive; at another outpost, a chap known as Two-Gun Steve had seven hundred pounds stolen. He set out to discover the thief, and eventually ran a native to earth in his hut. Without a moment's hesitation he dashed in, to find the native armed with a large knife of the type used for cutting away the scrub. Before he could protect himself, the native slashed at his head twice, missing it but cutting both shoulder muscles, so that he could not raise his arms. Diving at the native, he managed to knock him over and lie on him, then a native woman, hearing his yells, came into the hut and taking the revolver from his belt attempted to shoot the struggling native, but instead hit Steve in the stomach. Such was his vitality, however, that he managed to get hold of the gun and put two bullets into the native's stomach and a third into his head.

# Chapter 21 ~ Ghana ~ Burkina Faso ~ Mali ~ Algeria ~ Morocco

Pay day came at last, and I took my departure, going down at once to where I had left my car, and after a few days revelling in the sea and sailing with the Takoradi Yacht Club, I started off northward once more.

A report had come through of a small native rising, and one of the District Commissioners had been hit by a poisoned arrow, but I didn't see anything of this and got through without trouble. I made a call at Oda and was a guest of the great "Bogey" Newton, the manager of the W. A. D. S. [West African Diamond fields], or paddocks, as they call them here, who took me on a most interesting tour of inspection.

First we visited the magnetic separators which took out certain ores, then went to the long sheds where native women picked the diamonds out from what was left, working from small bowls half full of water. Gold was also being found in the same workings. Here the offices were literally paved with diamonds, as the material from which the concrete was made had been taken from the paddocks, and in one or two places, diamonds showed through which had not yet been removed.

Most of my camps were near native villages, and my staple food was yams and eggs washed down with tea. Often in the evening I would take the place of the local storyteller, and would perhaps try to tell them something about the "Queen Mary" but without much success, although they were too polite to say point-blank that they did not believe in the existence of a dugout large enough to hold all of them and their village houses as well.

At one point I came to a large river whose name I did not know and found a number of cattle bogged up to the nose in mud, so got a gang of boys and, with the assistance of the car, managed to pull most of them out.

I got hold of an old metal pontoon which was to be used in the construction of a new bridge after the rains, and had great difficulty getting the car on board.

Luckily, there were a number of planks, also intended for use in the construction of the bridge, and using these as a ramp I got on board after four hours' work, the boys often sinking up to their armpits in the muddy banks.

The crossing was made by tying a long creeper rope high up on the far bank and swinging across on the current. Here another difficulty cropped up; the bank was far too steep for the car to climb under its own power, but, getting a number of boys at the end of a long tow rope, I got into the driving seat, and giving them the word to pull, accelerated. However, the loose boards on the pontoon flew from under the wheels, and although I landed on the bank, I was slowly slipping back into the river. It is curious how quickly one's mind works in such an emergency; it was just about time to jump, but I figured that the car would take a few moments to sink and I could then jump for deep water and be picked up by one of the dugouts clear of the mud, while it was worth holding on, as it would be a devil of a job to get the car out again. Just then the rear wheels struck on a root and held. Something particularly funny now occurred; I sent one of the boys, who was holding onto the rope, to fetch everyone from a small village close by, and having got all the villagers on the rope and the engine just revving, I started to give the natives a chant lead, knowing they would give a terrific pull on the shouted response. All this time the car was at an angle of fort-five degrees. Off I started with my song, and I had just got to the part where the yell came in, when a wasp stung me on the leg. Down went my foot hard on the accelerator, and I let out a terrific yell, which made the natives leap into vigorous action, so that we came up the bank into safety.

The road continued to be bad until I reached a small village before Tamale, and here, while stopping in the resthouse, I had a puncture. Two of the United Africa Company's drivers offered to repair the small leak in the tyre while I had a lie-down, as it was terrifically hot. Presently one of the drivers appeared at the door and announced in a pained voice, "Master, this tyre not be good," producing the tyre in two halves. However, another one was eventually obtained.

In Tamale itself the heat was even greater, and there was not a breath of air, so that smoke from my pipe hung in a cloud round my head. The few natives I saw were very primitive and wore only small strips of hide and carried very long spears. Their villages were curious; a number of huts whose walls were built of red clay with thatched roofs were joined together by a clay wall in which small chambers were formed for the storage of grain.

At Navarongo, the last British post in Ghana, I found the District Commissioner down with a bad dose of malaria, but could do nothing for him and had to leave him lying there with the dry hot wind of the *harmattan* [a dry and dusty wind from the Sahara] blowing, filling the air with a pall of dust that blotted out the sun.

My route passed into French territory once more at Pol, where hundreds of natives sat outside the grey fort with its drooping tricolour waiting to pay duty on the chickens they had in their long wooden crates. I reported at the fort and the officer in charge telephoned the administrative centre at Ouagadougou, and I was allowed to proceed. At the outskirts of Ouagadougou I was stopped by a native policeman who insisted on accompanying me to the authorities. The conversation went something like this:-

Policeman: "+ *xx* - *!!!?*"

Self: "*Bon; toujours le commandant!*" [Good, always the commander!]

This seemed to defeat him, so he leapt on his pushbike and motioned me to follow him. Going slowly through the winding streets lined with mud houses, I saw a car approaching and suddenly remembering that I should be on the right-hand side and not the left, swerved across, nearly sweeping my escort off the face of the earth. However, he went gaily on, yelling at the populace to clear the road, and eventually fell exhausted at the office of the chief of police, being immediately succoured with water. I went in and produced my passport, and before I knew where I was it was stamped and returned and I was told to go to the Customs.

The native in charge of Customs didn't seem to speak French very well, so back I went to the police who produced another form to be signed, giving full details even down to my mother's maiden name, which had been overlooked on my previous visit. My escort once more leapt on his bicycle to direct me to Customs again, but just as I got into the car I was called back; a 'phone message having come through to say the man in charge of Customs had gone off to lunch. My guide, however, under the impression that I was behind him, went happily on down the road, then finding me missing, peddled back and again fell on the steps.

I then went to the Commandant, who spoke no English at all. I followed quite well his torrent of rapid French but behaved like Brer Rabbit, as I gathered they wanted me to pay duty, then had an inspiration and asked in deliberately execrable French to see the Governor. I was told that he didn't live in this part of the world at all, so I suggested wiring him the news of my arrival, which created an excellent impression. They paid for the wire, and I had no further trouble.

The walls of the Hotel Archambault, where I stayed the night, were decorated with painted frescoes. A huge Negro occupied the centre of the picture, while buxom white women danced round him. While I was at the hotel, natives offered me merchandise of all kinds ranging from spears to sandals, and among other things, I bought an almost fully-grown tame cheetah.

The *harmattan* was still blowing, causing a fog-like atmosphere and the natives I met were grey from the heavy dust-clouds. In the evening I managed to shoot a number of duck in close-by water holes, but found I could not keep pace with the cheetah's appetite, so I had to give him away in one of the villages.

The evenings were lonely without Congo or the cheetah and, having got my log up to date and my pipe going well, I had for my sole companions the spiders who burrowed in the sand, throwing up tiny clouds of dust as they formed small craters, or if I was in bush country, the monkeys who, filled with curiosity, would hang round the camp.

The country was particularly dry and flat and covered with thick coarse grass, and I had a bad moment running through a fierce grass fire that formed a line across my route. Water was very scarce even at the villages, but I managed to fill one water tank at Fada N'gourma and the other at Say.

Coming to the fast-flowing Niger, I had great difficulty in attracting the attention of the ferry, which was on the other side, but when I had done so, found it an efficient affair. The natives, however, had to paddle a mile and a half upstream to cross the swift current before they could land me at Niamey.

Following the north bank of the River Niger, I was on the fringe of the Sahara, but the narrow belt of trees along the water's edge gave me some protection from the sun. However, the nights which I spent in awful bat-infested resthouses, were bitterly cold.

At one point I had to get a working party, who were constructing a road, to push me, owing to the very soft sand, but then got into Gao without serious trouble. Here I started making preparations for the long Sahara crossing before me, having great trouble in this treeless area in finding planks of wood, which I should need to put under the car to prevent sinking in the sand, and eventually having to fall back on the lids of packing cases.

I intended to do the journey solo and without a guide, but in the morning just before I was ready to leave, one of the officials came across from the aerodrome there with a telegram from one of the stations up the river, asking me whether I would wait for another party of English people who were also wishing to cross. It seemed well while waiting, although I thought their large American car would be too fast for me in the desert.

While I was waiting, a private plane landed with an Italian pilot and an Englishwoman as passenger. We had meals in the same room, but as we had not been introduced, we didn't speak to each other, although we were the only English people within five hundred miles.

Later, the people who had wired arrived at Gao and proved to be a man and his wife. As they did not wish to take any risks in the desert, we took one of the native guides who rode in my car.

We left Gao, myself and the guide leading, and soon picked up the first of the faded red and white markers which were stuck on the tops of posts about fifteen feet high. These stretched in a line towards the horizon about five miles apart. Our route, however, was mainly controlled by the huge clumps of mercouba grass, some of it over two feet in height and matted with sand, over which we had to bump. In spite of this, the first day's run took us through to Tabankort. Here a lonely sous-officier made us welcome and was obviously very glad to see us. As it was still daylight, he asked me to take several photographs of himself and his camels and pigeons and to give them to his girl friend when I passed through Paris.

That evening, we slept outside the fort in huts made of woven grass matting. Before we turned in, we watched the sunset from the tower of the fort. The sky turned a deep indigo and the horizon a rich blood-red flecked with small golden clouds, and the camels at the foot of the wall below were bathed in the glow of the last sunrays.

Filling our tanks to the brim at the Ta-Brichat well, which was on top of a small hill, we set off, that day's run taking us only a hundred miles, as we stuck many times in the soft patches. In these patches we had to put planks under the rear wheels to enable them to get a grip, and having got moving again and run out onto harder ground, we would walk back for our planks, but often could not find them as they were already sunk in the soft sand. While digging with my hands for these I came across the amazing find of a pair of trousers, which our guide immediately appropriated.

This stretch was often very gruelling work, as one car would often get through these soft patches and have to go probably a mile before it came to ground firm enough to stop on, and the occupants would then have to walk back to the other car to help to push it out. This was easier in bare feet, as one's shoes always filled with sand. On the other hand the sand was too hot to walk on comfortably, so that usually one took off one's shoes and ran for a while, then put them on and walked the rest of the way.

The track wound about to avoid sand dunes and ridges, and I understand that this route is no longer used, another one having been started further to the east.

The night was bitterly cold, and the water we used for washing at night, and of course saved for future use in the radiator, was frozen in the morning. The cars were very difficult to start, and it was necessary to wrap rags that had been dipped in boiling water round the carburettors before the first kick could be got out of them.

From here the surface improved and stretched away in a long, level, hard, sandy plain on which the two cars raced, occasionally circling round and round each other for amusement. As we were passing no stationary objects by which speed could be judged, one had an extraordinary impression of flying.

*Bidon Cinque - Sahara*

160

Towards evening, a dark speck on the horizon indicated that we were getting near Bidon Cinque. This spot gets its name from having been the fifth petrol dump from the coast and it is now one of the best-known of the desert stops, although it consists only of two motor bus bodies with bunks inside and a petrol pump.

It is usually considered one of the most lonely spots in the world, but by great good luck, a French aeroplane had just landed as we arrived, and there were also three lorries belonging to the Shell Company who had come to erect an aeroplane beacon.

*Beacon - Sahara*

They had been there some days and their tents contained many luxuries such as an ice-chest for the daytime and a large oil stove for the night. They hospitably asked us to eat with them, and we all spent a very enjoyable evening together. The desert bus arrived at dusk, and when we went out to see what passengers it had on board, I tripped over the wireless aerial which they had just thrown up, and so broke off the news of their safe arrival which they were sending to Gao.

The desert still stretched away in endless flat yellow sand without a tuft of grass or a stone, and our speed was reduced by a terrific headwind. One afternoon, we had a bad scare when we found that, owing to this wind, our petrol consumption had nearly doubled, so we got behind one of the large sheet metal shed-like structures, which marked the route now that we were in Algeria, out of the wind, and decided that if necessary, I should let the other car have my supply of petrol and they would drive into

Reggan and send back further supplies. We tried driving at night when the wind dropped but found that although there was a full moon, we could not pick up the markers, as they were over six miles apart. Next day we again checked our petrol supply, and while we were doing so, a plane dived down out of the heat-haze. Without thinking, we both waved that we were O.K. and it disappeared again without knowledge of our petrol shortage which it could have reported for us.

*Central Sahara*

The cars were getting more difficult to start every morning, and my companions were getting very nervy. I had discovered that he was an Englishman born in Tunis and was a Mohommedan, as was his demure little wife, more I think from force of circumstances than from conviction, though she had much more of the fatalism of the Mohommedan than he had.

The petrol in one car ran out about five miles from Reggan, but by taking some from the other car we both managed to get to the brown walls of the fort. It was then getting dusk, and with the wind howling round it was extremely difficult to make those inside hear and let us in. When we got inside, I for one, thoroughly enjoyed a large dish of cous-cous with plenty of red wine, though I was considerably bothered by billions of house-flies.

In the morning we left on what was an actual track and, passing through the palms of the oasis and between the mounds of sand which marked the chain of wells that drained from one to another to fill a central one, we gradually started to climb the first foothills of the Atlas. Our track wended its way over bare hills and valleys strewn with large boulders and nowhere was there any sign of vegetation. Later, to the east, the huge sand dunes that form the Great Western Erg [a field of sand dunes in the Sahara, also called the Sand Sea] came into view with their sharp razor edges, and later still we came to small forts round which there was a little vegetation. These were often the outposts of the Foreign Legion. Many of them had a few miserable-looking houses clustering round the walls, the whole being surrounded by a barrier of barbed wire, a strip of which was removed by wild, rough-looking soldiers to allow us to enter.

After Colomb-Bechar the route became better defined, and the colour changes of the country were extraordinary, from jet-black volcanic rock to the brilliant yellow of the serrated sand hills of the Great Erg. As we travelled towards the northern seaboard, we found the villages becoming more prosperous; most of the houses, with their flat roofs, boasted a coat of whitewash, while gay *estaminets* [French cafes] stood at every corner. Bewhiskered Foreign Legionnaires swaggered along the streets eyeing the white prostitutes who sat at tables outside the cafes.

At one town I visited the Legion barracks and met an English Legionnaire called Allen. He told me that fifty-four percent of the Legion were Germans and the rest a mixture of French and every other nation. Their pay was sixty-four francs every fifteen days, while their quarters were comfortable, and these barracks had their own cinema. I did not envy him his lot, although he told me he would probably join up for another term of five years.

My companion in the other car spoke French and Arabic fluently, and conversed so volubly with the inhabitants of the various forts and villages, and especially with the Legionnaire officers, whom he invited to drink with him, that we were always hours late in leaving. Unfortunately it had been arranged that I should pay for the entertainment of the people we met and we should divide the 'exes' [slang for costs] when we parted, and this caused very bad blood between us, for when I presented the account he disputed the amount, not realising how quickly francs add up.

Between towns, desert conditions still existed, and I shall always remember the oppressive silence when the engines of the cars stopped for the night and the brilliant stars seemed to hang down just above our heads. It was still bitterly cold, but I found that the tufts of grass which were making their appearance and which had been packed into hard chunks by the sand which had blown into them, smouldered excellently when soaked in petrol and gave out a good warmth.

We were now climbing the Atlas Mountains and were beginning to see sparse vegetation, while many of the rocks were covered with a small and very green lichen.

As we got to the summit, the country was clothed in deep heather which supported hundreds of very woolly sheep, and later we camped among a circle of peaks on a vast sweet-smelling sage-covered plateau. We had lost all count of time, but worked out that this would be Christmas Day, and that evening we opened a tinned Christmas pudding I had carefully carried with me from the coast for the occasion. We poured a very small drop of cognac over it and set it alight, then wished each other a merry Christmas before crawling under the blankets for protection against the bitter wind.

By now we had crossed into Morocco and were among the gaily-dressed gipsy-like inhabitants, many of whom had tattooed foreheads and huge earrings. The men were rather a poor lot, and would steal anything if they got the chance.

We could now see the waters of the Mediterranean ahead in the distance and were running through beautiful scenery on tarred roads, passing lovely hill towns perched on the mountain slopes, catching glimpses of the inhabitants and recording mental images that will always remain, such as the lithe Arab boy mounted on a superb grey barb serenading his lady love, who took her ease dressed in many-hued clothes on her balcony overhanging the white froth of a bubbling stream, or the girls who leant from their windows calling to one another and flirting with the passers-by, or the Arabs ambling along with their *burnouses* pulled over their heads, the long folds almost concealing the minute donkeys on which they rode.

Cars were now making their appearance, and one which was approaching us at a terrific pace suddenly lost a wheel and shot off the road into a tree. I ran over and pulled the two occupants out, to find them badly cut about the face, and I had started to clean and bandage one of them when another car turned up and the driver began to attend to the other casualty. To me he seemed to making a pretty bad job of it, so I told him to stop and let me do it; his companion, however, informed me that he was an internationally known surgeon who was on holiday here, so I left the job to him.

Arriving in Oran, my car attracted a great deal of attention, and so did I whenever I got out of it, as the only clothes I had left were a pair of knee-length red native boots, a pair of shorts, a brilliantly coloured shirt, and a large wideawake hat. The kids rushed after me down the street with cries of "*Vive l'Americain!*" I think a cowboy film had just been shown in the town.

The traffic in Oran was terrible after our clear run, and my companions were in a complete dither by the time we got to a hotel. Here I parted with them after a hell of a row over the question of expenses, and I am afraid they still think they were done, although actually I was the loser.

# Chapter 22 ~ Algeria ~ Morocco ~ Gibraltar ~ Spain ~ England

From Oran I made a run through what must be some of the finest scenery in the world, going back onto the Atlas and then coming down to the coast again at Algiers, where I visited the British Consulate and was invited to the New Year's Eve festivities, feeling overjoyed at meeting English people again.

The following day I was down with another violent dose of malaria, and while I was convalescing from this, under the kind care of Captain and Mrs. de Malglaive, who had made a name for themselves racing small British cars, I visited many of the beauty spots of Algiers, including the Garden of Allah.

Before leaving Algiers I also visited the Casbah during the feast of Ramadan. After the evening signal had gone, the small cafes were crowded to overflowing with people breaking their long fast. In the narrow streets that wind up the hillside on which the native part is built, the houses in many places met above the footways and in others the leaning tops were only two feet apart to admit a glimpse of the star-spangled sky. The scene would have inspired an artist. The lower parts of the houses were mostly brothels, and over a broken wall showed a house painted pale blue, from each window of which, as well as from the ornate door, gaily-dressed women, looking like Spanish beauties in the dim light, beckoned and called, while Arabs, Berbers, French and Italian sailors, and Spanish in brilliant blue and red, passed up and down the narrow ways to the curiously detached music of a hidden native band.

I wandered from place to place, all of them garishly decorated; here a band of very fat naked women danced an endless can-can, there men, obviously under the influence of drugs, shuffled round and round to the sound of a mechanical piano, and high up in the pale pink wall, under an old Moorish lamp, a hag with her head swathed in a bright scarf and wearing long earrings, looked through a small window and mouthed horribly at the dancers.

Before I left I had an amusing experience with the Preventive officers. Coming back late at night with the car still fully loaded with my kit, I was descending a steep hill with my lights blazing, having no dippers. I saw a car at the bottom, so I stopped and turned out my lights so that they would not be blinded, but as they did not move, I proceeded again, and after I had passed them I found they were following me. I stopped to let them go by, which they did, but only travelled slowly ahead of me and then pulled round broadside across the road and I nearly crashed into them, as my brakes were very much worn. Four Preventive officers then tumbled out and demanded to be allowed to search my kit, as they thought I was smuggling. I had not emptied the car since crossing the desert, and I still had on board a number of gin bottles containing water which I had stuck in odd corners as a reserve supply. They came across these and one by one they took them out and stood them in a long line on the road, then solemnly tasted each one, and although they then let me continue they still seemed very suspicious.

Leaving Algiers, I lazed along the coast of the blue Mediterranean, staying at small native cafes set among flowering almond blossom and joking with the dark-eyed women. I paid a visit to Sidi Bel Abbes, the headquarters of the Foreign Legion, where I dined with the officers, who took me on a pub-crawl to watch Spanish cabaret dancers with their clicking castanets.

Then I passed through the interesting town of Fez and on into Spanish Morocco, and from there into the International Zone and Tangiers, where I was followed by crowds of small boys who chanted "Me nice boy, go to English school... show you naked woman - you like my sister - see Arab woman dance... You buy smutty post card?" And to this chorus I left Africa for the short run to Gibraltar.

*[Archie in Gibraltar, the same car, but a different trip]*

When I arrived there, the Hood and the Renown had just been in collision and had come into port, and there were some two thousand officers and ratings ashore, so the town was en fete. The cabarets were full, and it was amusing to see the ratings from the two ships discussing the collision, beer-mugs and match-boxes being used to represent the ships, while their courses were illustrated by dipping a finger in the beer and tracing a line on the top of the table. Some of the Gordon Highlanders, knowing nothing about nautical matters, were called in to arbitrate between the disputants, and only made matters worse, eventually being squashed by both sides as, "so-and-so land-lubbers" but all in the most friendly spirit.

While here I got in touch with the makers of my car and suggested that they might like to have it after its wonderful run. Without much enthusiasm they accepted the gift of the car and offered to pay for the cost of driving it home.

Just before leaving Gibraltar, I was approached by a Scotsman and an Irishman who said they were on a walking tour and would welcome a lift through Andalusia. Apparently the Irishman had spent his life in a monastery, but his health had broken down and he had been ordered to go on holiday.

Paddy was a particularly morose individual and apparently terrified of getting lost, so they would both follow close on my heels while I wandered round the towns. In Malaga they followed me into a cabaret and took seats next to me. The first turn was a particularly lewd dance by a nude Spanish girl, which completely finished poor Paddy, fresh from the monastery, and he hardly spoke again until we packed him off home from Madrid.

Many of the towns were holding a fiesta, and we got into a battle of flowers where crowds of excited people were throwing tough-looking chunks of grass sod at each other.

There seemed to be a state of general alarm and armed guards and police were everywhere, but I only saw three small boys arrested and handcuffed together. As we left, the sun was just touching the Gibral Faro (Moorish castle) that dominated the town from its position on the hill, then on we went through the gnarled trunks of the olive trees and over barren mountainous country to Madrid, then through the Monte de Montejo and Puerto de Somosierra, where the peaks were covered with snow.

Leaving Spain at San Sabastian, we made directly for Paris, travelling in a very heavy fall of snow, with only one stop to tow an Englishman's super car out of a snowdrift.

In Paris I was welcomed by the Austin agent, who said "*Monsieur*, a wonderful ride! I no spik English, so I get two nice girl and plenty champagne, yes? Good?" It was.

The Paris papers came out the following morning with an account of my adventures, but still I was not an explorer. They described me as, "*un chasseur, mais un chasseur d'une extreme modestie*" ["a hunter, but an extremely modest hunter"]. So they couldn't have understood all my French.

The run to Boulogne was without incident, and the Scotsman left me to join the Foreign Legion, whose recruiting offices were at Dunkirk, but I afterwards heard that he never got there. On my next trip to Africa, I was giving a broadcast in Jo'burg when he rang me up.

An uneventful passage landed me at Folkestone which I had left nearly four years before.

Mr. Lee of the Austin Company met me, and we went on an extensive pub-crawl to London. The following day the car was on show in Oxford Street beside a very inaccurate map showing my journey.

Anyhow, I did better than the man who brought his boots back to the makers - although it cost the car manufacturers quite a lot for expenses through Europe, I made an additional profit of seven pounds.

I had done over thirty-seven thousand miles and arrived back with a clear profit of two pounds more than I had had when I first conceived the idea.

And was I an explorer? Here's an extract from the "Times", published in a fit of enthusiasm as I neared home:-

*"A British motorist, Mr. A. E. Filby, of Bromley, Kent, has arrived at Algiers on the last stage of a tour round Africa in a seven-year old car. - Reuter."*

A visit to the Club produced a new member who walked round the car with flattering interest and then said, "By Jingo, you must have had a tough time," and I, with a tale of adventure waiting to be tapped, "Oh, not too bad." "But how did you get on for fresh milk every day?"

This seemed an anti-climax, but worse was to follow. I went into the hall, where Styles, the perfect hall-porter, greeted me with, "Morning, Sir. Have you had a nice holiday? There are a few letters for you. They look like bills."

I went into the bar for inspiration.


**A E Filby**
**1938**

# Epilogue ~ A tragic love story

Archie, having arrived in England, was already planning another round trip to Cape Town, again by car, but this time blazing a trail down the west coast of Africa and returning along the east. This he successfully completed. Ultimately he would cross the Sahara seven times, once on his own.

By now he was quite famous and being heralded as 'the World's most travelled motorist'. He was much in demand on radio and television. In one BBC radio broadcast, 'In Town Tonight', Mrs Patricia Byron, another globe-trotter, described a dramatic rescue. She was stranded in the heart of the Sahara, an area larger than the United States, and two hundred miles from the nearest town. Whether or not she was alone is uncertain. Suddenly, through the heat-haze, a decrepit motor vehicle appeared, manned by a sand-and-wind swept individual. He repaired her radiator, allowing her to continue her journey, and frankly saved her life. It was none other than my Uncle Archie.

A week later, and by popular demand, Archie appeared again on the same BBC radio programme.

Page 4.—DAILY SKETCH

# Bee-Sting Started Radio Romance

WHEN Mr. A. Filby, the author-explorer, sets out soon to cross the Sahara for the eighth time and traverses four continents in a car, he will take a bride with him—thanks to a B.B.C. broadcast and an amazing chain of coincidences.

"It began with a bee-sting on my face." Mrs. Filby—Miss Fay Taylor, authoress, globe-trotter — told a DAILY SKETCH reporter last night.

Mr. Filby explained to me:

"We met out in Singapore 12 years ago. I have not stayed in one country for as long as three months in 20 years.

"She was a girl of 16, travelling with her parents. We became friends, but never corresponded or met again till last July.

"Then I broadcast on my adventures.

Fay was listening, because a bee-sting on the face had changed her plans and made her stay in town for the week-end.

"She recognised my voice, rang up the B.B.C.

"In the ordinary way I should have left the building, but I had met an old friend from Australia, who stopped me on the doorstep of Broadcasting House for a chat.

"I was just setting off when a breathless commissionaire ran to say I was wanted on the telephone.

"The result of that was a meeting. And the result of the meeting was a wedding two months ago.

"We're going out together this time—writing, exploring, studying."

Mr. and Mrs. Filby will broadcast together on Saturday.

169

One listener, Miss Fay Taylor, recognised the voice of a man she had met in the Far East, twelve years earlier, when she was a girl of sixteen. It was by chance that Fay heard the broadcast, having been stung by a bee, and changing her plans, had stayed at home. She telephoned the BBC and she and Archie met up again. They renewed their friendship, which blossomed into romance, and were married in Kingston, Surrey, on the 7th October 1938.

*Fay*

Both Fay and Archie were now invited to relate their story on BBC Radio and Television.

*Archie and Fay*

In 1939, Archie and Fay continued travelling abroad together, until September when World War II broke out. Both applied to work in any capacity designated by the War Office and both were posted to Iceland. In 1941, Archie successfully applied for a transfer to West Africa, an area he was intimate with. Fay would follow him after a three-month ship voyage, via Canada and the United States.

Arriving at Freetown, Sierra Leone, Uncle Archie assumed his duties at the British Naval Base. Whilst waiting for Fay, he narrowly missed seeing his younger brother, my father, who was being transported to Burma and whose ship was one of many moored in the Freetown harbour. Archie commandeered a rowing boat and made a valiant but unsuccessful attempt to find his younger brother. They never saw each other again.

Disaster struck. Already prone to recurring bouts of malaria, Archie succumbed to one final violent attack. He fell into a coma from which he never recovered, and died on 8 October 1942. He was 42 years old. Fay arrived in Freetown *one day too late*.

Died of Blackwater Fever

in Military Hospital at

FREETOWN.SIERRA LEONE.W.AFRICA

Eighth October 1942 .

Fay stayed on at the Naval Base in Sierra Leone, and in 1944 sent the following letter home: (see overleaf)

In a final family volume, Archie's father briefly mentions that Fay remarried "at a little old church, Freetown" in 1945, but to whom and what became of the couple is not known.

~~~~~~~~

c/o British Council,
P.O. Box 124,
Freetown,
Sierra Leone,
W.Africa.

8th April, 1944.

Mummie darling,

This is just a very brief line to say
how sorry I am for not having written for
a long time. The fact is that I've recently changed my job, and am now so continually on the run that I thought I'd
put off writing to you until I got time
to do it in peace. However, there seems
to be no prospect that that will ever
happen, so I'll just have to dash off a
few words on this perfectly dreadful old
machine.

The new job is interesting. You may
have heard of the British Council. It
used to be called The British Council for
Cultural Something-or-Other, and was
started in 1933, mainly to put the British
point of view across in a non-political
way in countries that didn't know much
about us, by way of a counter to the very
active Nazi propaganda agencies that
were functioning so busily everywhere.
When the war began, that had to shut
down in a good many places, and then
someone had the bright idea that our
own Colonies didn't really know an
awful lot about us, so the Council decided to start operations all over the

Empire. Out here it's particularly necessary and a particularly uphill job.
We hope to give people, both European
and African, some opportunity to do

something with their minds when the day's
work is over. As it is they've nothing
to do but visit each other and xxx go to
a few pictures or dances occasionally.
We've already xxx run one or two lectures
and have planned some more; we hope to
start a gramophone club and an art class,
and I am going to teach classical dancing
to some young African schoolmistresses.
There's a good deal of office work to
be done as well as all this, so I'm
just about run to death. Still, it's
more fun than helping to control
Road Transport.

Goodness only knows when I'll get
any leave, but that's not bothering me
very much. I'm quite fond of Freetown
and don't mind much how long I stay
here.

God bless, darling. Love to
everyone,

Fay

P.S. There is now an Airgraph service
to this place for civilians. It saves
a lot of time. Ask about it at a Post
Office. The Air Mail things Father sends
are simply sent to me by sea mail.

~~~~~~~

# The HORIZON FEVER Series

Of course the African expedition described in *Horizon Fever* is just one of my uncle's many 'jaunts'. I'm delighted to say that his scrapbooks, stuffed with anecdotes and photographs, have allowed us to plan another two books in the *Horizon Fever* series:

~~~~~

## Horizon Fever II - Australasia Calling

A E Filby's account, with photographs, of his adventures in Australia, New Zealand and beyond. In this book, Archie describes how he became a miner, a buckjumper, a racing driver, a pearl diver, a convicted felon and finally brought his partner home "tied up; a raving lunatic."

~~~~~~~~

## Horizon Fever III - Seven Crossings of the Sahara Desert

A E Filby's account, with photographs, of his seven extraordinary crossings of the Sahara desert, one of which he completed alone.

~~~~~~~~

*If you would like advance notice of when these two titles are launched, or would like to contact us with comments or questions, please email us at Vicky@VictoriaTwead.com. We'd love to hear from you!*

~~~~~~~~

# More Books

## Chickens, Mules and Two Old Fools
Victoria Twead

Perhaps if Joe and Vicky had known what relocating to a tiny village tucked in the Alpujarra mountains would really be like, they might have hesitated... They have no idea of the culture shock in store. No idea they will become reluctant chicken farmers and own the most dangerous cockerel in Spain. No idea they will be befriended by an 85 year old spliff-smoking sex-kitten, help capture a vulture or be rescued by a mule. Life is never dull as they embark on their Five Year Plan.

Vicky and Joe's story is packed with irreverent humour, animals, eccentric characters and sunshine.

*'A truly hilarious page-turner.'*

*"Weeks later you will be doing the dishes and recall some fleeting scene with chickens or mules or two old fools and laugh out loud all over again."* **The Catalunya Chronicle**

*"a charming and funny expat tale"* **The Telegraph, UK**

Paperback and Ebook editions available from Amazon.

# Two Old Fools - Olé!
## Victoria Twead

Vicky and Joe have finished fixing up their house and look forward to peaceful days enjoying their retirement. Then the fish van arrives, and instead of delivering fresh fish, disgorges the Ufarte family. The peace of El Hoyo is shattered.

Packed with badly behaved humans and animals, irreverent humour and sunshine, 'Two Old Fools - Olé!' will make you laugh out loud, while the mouth-watering Spanish recipes will have you reaching for your saucepan.

*"I absolutely loved it! Funny, honest and impossible to put down."* **Justin Aldridge, Eye on Spain**

Paperback and Ebook editions available from Amazon.

~~~~~~~~~

**Two Old Fools on a Camel**
Victoria Twead

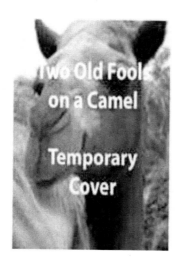

The continuing story of Joe and Victoria as they leave Spain for the Middle East, as the Arab Spring erupts.

(Estimated launch: early 2013)


Paperback and Ebook editions will be available from Amazon.


~~~~~~~~

# Mouth-Watering Spanish Recipes
## Victoria Twead and Gayle Macdonald

At last! A cookbook packed with colour photos and easy step-by-step instructions for preparing delicious Spanish dishes, both traditional and unusual. Victoria Twead and Gayle Macdonald have combined their passion for Spanish food to compile this cookbook, guaranteed to bring Spanish sunshine into your kitchen.

What could be healthier, more colourful or tastier than the Mediterranean style of cooking? This book has it all: tapas, paella, barbecue, seafood, meat, salads, vegetarian, drinks, desserts and much more. In addition to more than 100 mouth-watering recipes, there are fascinating articles about Spanish cooking and the authors' experiences of living in Spain.

Ingredients are shown in both metric and US measures.

*"Easy to use - superb lay-out with a very comprehensive list of authentic recipes and quality photographs, this book truly defines 'mouth-watering'."* Amazon review.

Ebook edition available from Amazon.

~~~~~~~~

***Morgan and the Martians - A Comedy Play-Script for Children***
Victoria Twead

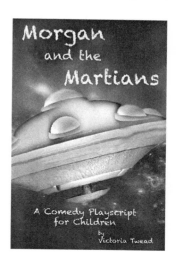

Morgan is a bad boy. A VERY bad boy. When a bunch of Martians give him a Shimmer Suit that makes him invisible, he wastes no time in wearing it to school and creating havoc. Well, wouldn't you?

This English comedy drama will amuse and encourage the most reluctant of readers, and will fire fertile young imaginations. Teachers will find the accompanying Resource Pack a godsend, both as part of a syllabus or an end-of-term filler.

Suitable for KS2 or ages 7 to 11. Includes FREE printable classroom assignments.

*"Excellent way of getting kids interested in reading, and develop their imagination and creativity."* Amazon review.

Paperback and Ebook editions available from Amazon.

~~~~~~~

# Contact and Links

The Austin 20 that Archie drove on his African exploration is owned by the National Motor Museum. It has featured in their Feats of Endurance exhibition, and can be seen on display at the museum in Beaulieu, Brockenhurst, Hampshire.

**http://www.nationalmotormuseum.org.uk/**

Archie's photographs from *Horizon Fever*, plus many extras that did not fit into the book, can be found on **Pinterest**.
**http://pinterest.com/victoriatwead/**

Connect with Victoria at this email address:
**TopHen@VictoriaTwead.com**

Facebook: **https://www.facebook.com/VictoriaTwead**

Victoria's Website and Blog: **http://www.VictoriaTwead.com**

Free Stuff and Village Updates monthly newsletter and draw:
**http://bit.ly/5U9F2k**

# From Archie's Scrapbook

This is the mock-up for a magazine advertisement that featured Archie, proclaiming the wonders of Punchbowle Pipe Tobacco.

*"I have just completed a safari of 37,000 miles that took me across the dryness of the Sahara, down to the humidity of the West Coast of Africa, through South-West Africa, to return via the French Sudan where temperatures were somewhere about 112° in the shade... Wherever opened, Punchbowle was always tobacco at its very best... The picture shows me testing for a crossing over a flooded river in Angola."*

# MAP OF AFRICA

*This map shows Archie's route through Africa - running clock-wise from Egypt, all the way down to South Africa, and up the other side of the continent.*

Lightning Source UK Ltd.
Milton Keynes UK
UKOW05f0113250214

227072UK00002BA/434/P